Inviting God In

Also by Rabbi David Aaron

*Endless Light: The Ancient Path
of the Kabbalah to Love, Spiritual
Growth, and Personal Power*

*Seeing God: Ten Life-Changing
Lessons of the Kabbalah*

*The Secret Life of God:
Discovering the Divine within You*

Inviting God In

CELEBRATING
—— THE ——
SOUL-MEANING
—— OF THE ——
JEWISH
HOLY DAYS

—— ❦ ——

Rabbi David Aaron

Trumpeter   *Boston & London*   2006

Trumpeter Books
An imprint of Shambhala Publications, Inc.
Horticultural Hall
300 Massachusetts Avenue
Boston, Massachusetts 02115
www.shambhala.com

9 8 7 6 5 4 3 2

Printed in the United States of America

Designed by Graciela Galup

♾ This edition is printed on acid-free paper that meets the
American National Standards Institute Z39.48 Standard.
Distributed in the United States by Random House, Inc., and in
Canada by Random House of Canada Ltd

Library of Congress Cataloging-in-Publication Data
Aaron, David, 1957–
Inviting God in: celebrating the soul-meaning of the Jewish holy
days/David Aaron.—1st ed.
p.   cm.
ISBN-13: 978-1-59030-337-5 (alk. paper)
ISBN-10: 1-59030-337-7
1. Fasts and feasts—Judaism.   2. God—Judaism.   3. Spiritual
life—Judaism.   I. Title.
BM690.A14   2006
296.4′3—dc22
2006000830

Special thanks to my true friend Dr. Herb Caskey, whose generosity made this project possible. May the study of these secrets bring great merit to his parents, Morris and Rose Caskey of blessed memory.

To my fabulous parents, Joseph and Luba

To my phenomenal wife, Chana

To my amazing children, Lyadia, Aaron, Ne'ema,
Ananiel, Nuriel, Yehuda, Tzuriel, and Shmaya

To my sweet grandchildren, Nachalya & Shira

Contents

Acknowledgments

Great thanks to my wife, Chana. May each day of our lives be a joyous and constant celebration of our love for God, each other, our parents, children, and all people.

Many, many thanks to my very talented editor, Elicia Mendlowitz, who did an exceptional job helping me put these ideas into writing. I am also very thankful to Uriela Sagiv for adding her professional touch, giving these ideas even greater clarity.

My deep appreciation to Beth Frankl of Trumpeter Books for her expertise and advice.

I am extremely grateful to the many friends and supporters of Isralight International, whose generosity has provided me with the opportunity to present the ideas of this book. Special thanks to Dr. Herb Caskey, Robby and Helene Rothenberg, Andrew and Shannon Penson, Dr. Michael and Jackie Abels, George and Pam Rohr, David and Dena Reiss, Robyn Barsky, Tzvi Fishman, and Steve Eisenberg for their consistent love and support.

I am also grateful to the many students who have attended my talks, Isralight seminars, and retreats. Your questions, challenges, and receptivity have brought me much blessing and inspiration.

I am forever in debt to my holy teachers, especially Rabbi Shlomo Fischer *shlita*, for all their brilliance and warmth.

Thank you, God. My entire being is filled with joy and gratitude to serve You.

David Aaron
Old City, Jerusalem

Author's Note

In the Jewish tradition, God is never called God. God has many names, and how we refer to God depends on how we perceive a given encounter with the Divine Presence. But for the purposes of this book, I felt it necessary to use the word *God,* as this is the accepted English usage. Also, to avoid convoluted language, I reluctantly acceded to using the pronoun *He,* even though it can be very misleading and does not convey the full truth about God.

Introduction

It's a Holiday!

The comedian Henny Youngman once said, "I tried being an atheist, but I gave it up. There were no holidays." What is a holiday really about? Is it the same as a vacation? Decidedly not. A vacation is a time to vacate, but a holiday is a time to celebrate.

"To vacate" means taking off, getting away from the daily grind and its tensions and challenges. It means tanning on a beach, playing golf, or catching a good concert. A holiday, however, is something else. It is not an escape from everyday life to paradise. Rather, it is a time to infuse paradise into everyday life. That is why it is called a *holy* day—it is a day that is whole in every way, and that is cause to celebrate. For me the word *celebrate* evokes the word *celestial*. A Jewish holiday is a time to see the celestial within the terrestrial. It is a time to acknowledge how the divine enters our world and meets us in time.

A Jewish holiday is referred to in Hebrew as a *moed*. This actually means a "date" or a "meeting." In other words, a holiday is a date with God.

But why would we need to make a date with God? Even though my wife and I have been married for over twenty years, we regularly go out on dates. Although we see each other daily, our profound connection often gets overshadowed by the hustle and bustle of life. We know that life sometimes gets in the way of love, and we can forget how deep is our love for each other. The same goes for other aspects of life that people take for granted. When was the last time you noticed your breath or your heartbeat? Unless you lose your breath or miss a beat, these miracles of life often go unnoticed and unappreciated. It is precisely because they are constant and consistent that you forget them and lose the wonder they should inspire.

God is with us every moment of our life. Therefore, it is easy for us to forget that His presence fills the present. The holidays, however, mark special times in Jewish history when God's loving presence was dramatically obvious.

THE JEWISH DRAMA OF LIFE

I was once sitting and learning Torah with the Hollywood actor Kirk Douglas when suddenly he turned to me and said, "You know, Rabbi, I love being Jewish."

"Oh, yeah? Why?" I asked. "Because being Jewish is dramatic!" I was surprised by his unusual answer and thought to myself, "I guess for these big-time actors, everything is showbiz." Instead, I said, "Dramatic? I am sorry, but I don't get the connection." "Rabbi, I know drama, and let me tell you, Jewish life and Jewish history are dramatic. In fact, there are several archetypal themes to all films, and they are all from the Bible. Here, let me show you what's drama."

Kirk then jumped out of his chair and began to improvise a dramatic scene.

"Now, watch this. Let's say we are shooting a scene and it's about a guy named Jerry who is going to get some bad news about his mother. How do we make it dramatic? We would not have Jerry sitting at home reading a newspaper when suddenly the phone rings and someone breaks the news to him that his mother is fatally ill. No, that's not interesting—that's not dramatic. So, this is how it's done: First, Jerry is at a party. No, better yet, he's at a party in his honor—it's a big company event and he's about to receive an important award. Now, imagine he's wearing a tuxedo, he has a martini in his hand, and he's socializing with his friends at the reception before the event. He cracks a joke and then, in the middle of the laughter, someone hands him a note."

At this point, Kirk became Jerry, masterfully acting out the entire scene as Jerry casually glanced at the note, a pained look appeared on his smiling face, and he choked out in response to his friends' inquiring looks, "It's my mother."

After a few theatrical moments of silence, Kirk perked up and said with a big smile, "Now, that's drama! Get it, Rabbi?" "Kind of." "Drama happens in the sharp contrasts of life—between happiness and sadness, failure and success, defeat and victory, darkness and light. And that is the story of the Jewish people. It's dramatic." Kirk was right. And, in fact, all the Jewish holidays connect us with the drama of Jewish history, the sharp turns and striking contrasts of which inspire powerful clarity. Remembering what *was* in the past awakens us to see what *is* in the present and what *can be* in the future. In fact, the holidays empower us to recognize how God's love is with us all the time. This is the soul-meaning of the Jewish Holy Days. Each holiday celebrates a critical ingredient in the recipe for a loving relationship with God and our fellow human beings—freedom, responsibility, fallibility, accountability, forgiveness, spontaneity, integrity, wholeness, intimacy, anticipation, hope, and trust. Each holiday in the Jewish calendar is a date with God. Each holiday is an opportunity to relive the dramatic events that occurred on those days—to remember and celebrate God's timeless love for us. This is the soul-meaning of the Jewish Holy Days.

—ONE—

Passover

Celebrating
Unconditional Love

A story is told about a rabbi who wanted to show an atheist the folly of his disbelief in God. The rabbi turned a bottle of ink on its side so that it would drip onto a page of beautiful poetry. When the atheist came to visit the rabbi, the rabbi said, "You won't believe this, but the wind knocked over my inkwell and the ink spilled out a poem onto the paper." Of course, the fellow said, "Ridiculous. Such a random act is impossible. There is simply too much design and meaning to this poem for it to have been composed by accident." To that the rabbi responded, "Then how could you look at the world and believe that it is an accident?" Imagine if there were a thousand monkeys in a room, sitting for billions of years, banging away at the keyboards of a thousand computers. The chances that they would come up with three comprehensive words, let alone one cohesive sentence or paragraph, are incredibly slim. But that is basically the claim of a person who believes that the world is just an accident.

It seems obvious to most people that the world is the creation of an intelligent entity. However, it is not so obvious to most people that this intelligent entity is a *loving* entity. There could be a God who created us all, but how do we know that this creator, this ruling power, loves His creation?

The great scientist Albert Einstein believed that God "does not play dice with the universe," and therefore he sought to formulate the unified field theory that would make sense of creation. Einstein was sure that this universe is a manifestation of a creative intelligence. However, when asked what question remained unanswered for him, he answered that he would like to know if "the universe is friendly." How can we know that the force of creative intelligence responsible for the incredible design of the world is warm, personal, loving? How can we be sure that the force of creative intelligence cares about you and me?

There is no way for science to prove that the universe is friendly or that the force behind it all personally cares about His creation. Science can only show us that God is intelligent.

Jewish history, however, shows us that God loves us and cares. In fact, the holiday of Passover teaches us that God's love and care are unconditional.

IN THE NAME OF LOVE

Passover commemorates the miraculous Exodus of the Israelites from Egypt. After 210 years of oppression and cruel servitude, an entire nation of slaves left in astounding record time, faster than it takes dough to rise for bread. We celebrate this event with a festive ceremonial meal called a Seder, during which we recite the *Haggadah*—the retelling of this wondrous historic episode.

The Exodus from Egypt is not just another milestone in the history of the Jewish people. It is *the* milestone, *the* cornerstone, and *the* Rosetta stone. It is so important that every other holiday is actually a memorial to the Exodus. Even Shabbat is referred to as *Zechar L'Yitziat Mitzraim*, a "Remembrance of the Exodus from Egypt," although it has no apparent connection to the Exodus. In addition, every Jew is obligated to see himself or herself as having personally left Egypt and to recount this fact *every* day.

The first of the Ten Commandments plainly states, "I am YHVH (the Lord) your God who took you out of Egypt, out of the house of bondage." And it is explained in the *Zohar*, the magnum opus of the Jewish mystical tradition, better known as the Kabbalah: "This is the foundation and the root of Torah, of all the commandments, and of the complete faith of Israel."

Thus we see that the Exodus is considered the seminal event of the Jewish calendar and of daily Jewish consciousness.

Although the obvious theme of the holiday is freedom, it is commonly referred to as Passover. Wouldn't the "Holiday of Freedom" or the "Exodus" be more appropriate?

The Jewish tradition teaches that it is so named because God *passed over* the houses of the Israelites during the tenth and final plague when He caused the death of the Egyptian firstborn. This disturbing image of God, hopping and skipping over the Israelites' homes, is also found in the Song of Songs, which is read on Passover: "Behold the voice of my beloved comes skipping over the mountains, hopping over the valleys." The Jewish oral tradition emphasizes that the "beloved" was God Himself.

The Jerusalem Talmud teaches that God personally came to redeem the Israelites—He did not send an angel or some other agent. This is clearly stated in the book of Exodus, which reads, "*I* will perform judgment—I am *YHVH* (the Lord)." The famous eleventh-century Torah commentator Rashi explains that here God is assuring the Israelites, "I, Myself, and not an agent will deliver you from your oppression and enslavement."

But couldn't God have simply decreed the death of the firstborn without all this skipping around? What is the significance of His personal involvement?

It is common knowledge that the Israelites in Egypt deteriorated to the forty-ninth level of spiritual impurity and moral decadence. The Talmudic sages tell us that God saved them just before they fell to the last level, the fiftieth, which is total spiritual suicide and obliteration. In other words, the Israelites were actually unworthy of liberation. So why did God free them nonetheless?

A careful reading of the Exodus story shows that the predominant message of the liberation of the Israelites was the revelation of the profound truth of "I am YHVH."

> And *Elohim* [God] spoke to Moses and said: "I am YHVH [the Lord]; I appeared to Abraham, Isaac and Jacob, as *Shaddai* [the Almighty], but my name YHVH, I did not make known to them. (Exodus 6:2–3)

We know that each divine name used in the Torah indicates a different encounter with God, revealing different attributes and perspectives of the divine truth.

Elohim is God revealed as the Creator of nature, borders, rules, principles, and regulations. This is the name that appears throughout the creation story. In addition, this name refers to God when He is revealed as the Judge, committed to laws, order, justice, consequences, and cause and effect. God as Elohim responds measure for measure to the choices and deeds of people. Therefore, God as Elohim cannot save the Israelites, because they don't deserve it.

However, in the Exodus story God is not only referred to as Elohim, but also as YHVH. This divine name is mentioned when God's compassion is revealed. It indicates that God is not only the Creator, the Ruler, and the Judge, but also a compassionate Sustainer. He lovingly extends and shares His being with us, perpetuating our existence at every moment. We do not exist independently of YHVH; rather, we are unified with Him as the rays of the sun are always united with the sun or thoughts are always united with the thinker. Therefore, the name YHVH suggests that God is like a compassionate parent and we are His children.

A verse in the Psalms reads, "You are children unto YHVH, your *Elohim*." The Talmud records a discussion regarding the meaning of this verse. One Talmudic sage claims that we are considered children of God only when we conduct ourselves as His children. However, Rabbi Meir disagrees and insists, "Whether you do or don't, either way you are called God's children." The Talmud accepts the opinion of Rabbi Meir and proves that he is correct: "Did not the prophet Jeremiah call them 'foolish children'—foolish yet children? Did not Moses call them 'faithless children'—faithless yet children? So, too, the prophet Isaiah referred to them as 'descendants of evildoers, children that deal corruptly,' but nonetheless children. Even if they leave God completely and turn to idolatry, the prophet Hosea said that they are still destined to be called 'children of the living God.'"

THE LEAP OF LOVE

God as Elohim is committed to the laws of nature and only works within the limitations of time and space.

Therefore, God as Elohim could not liberate the Israelites from Egypt.

God as YHVH, however, is beyond nature. He is the miracle worker who, in the name of love, can transcend time and space and perform supernatural feats. Indeed, the Exodus of the Israelites was miraculous. The Egyptian military security was so tight that no slave had ever succeeded in escaping Pharaoh's captivity. And yet the entire nation of 600,000 households left Egypt in less time than it takes for dough to rise. To mobilize my own small family to leave the house takes longer than that. But they were able to get out so quickly because God suspended the laws of nature. And He not only suspended the laws of nature, but also the laws of justice. This, perhaps, is the greatest miracle in the Exodus story—that even though the Israelites were undeserving of being liberated by God as Elohim, they were nonetheless saved by God as YHVH.

Judaism teaches that YHVH—a name that is so holy we are forbidden to pronounce it—is the essential name of God, and that the essential attribute of God is love and compassion. This basic truth is embodied in the Exodus story, and this is why we must remember the Exodus daily.

The name Elohim is really only an aspect of the name YHVH. In other words, the divine attribute of justice is an aspect of the attribute of love but subordinate to it. This truth is expressed by the Shema, the central credo of Judaism: *Shema Israel, YHVH Eloheinu, YHVH ehad*— "Hear O Israel, YHVH, *our Elohim*, is the one and only

YHVH." In other words, we need to understand the deep truth that YHVH is Elohim while remaining YHVH. And, by extension, God's commitment to justice is actually an aspect of the full expression of His love.

Such is the way of true parenthood. Because of my love for my daughter, I establish for her rules and regulations. I create a world of law and order where her choices incur real consequences. I judge her, reward her, and discipline her, all for the sake of empowering her to take responsibility and live up to her potential. However, since my judgment is derived from my love (and thereby is subordinate to it), there may be times when I will be compassionate toward her even though she does not deserve it. I will "pass over" my standards of judgment—I will overrule my rules—in the name of love. This is the meaning of the verse in the Song of Songs: "Behold the voice of my beloved comes skipping over the mountains, hopping over the valleys." Nothing can stand in the way of God's love for us. No obstacle is too great. His love transcends all barriers.

This is the inner dynamic of the Exodus, and this is why the holiday that celebrates it is commonly referred to as Passover. God, in order to pass over the homes of the Israelites, passed over His attribute of judgment in the name of love. The *Zohar* teaches, "Even though God loves justice, His love for His children overcame His love for His justice."

We can now understand why God, so to speak, had to pull off the Exodus Himself and could not entrust an angel to do the job. According to the Jewish tradition, angels are bound to the laws of nature and the laws of justice. The great thirteenth-century Spanish Kabbalist Bachya ibn Halawa explains that had God sent an angel to unleash the plague of the firstborn, then even the Israelites would have died, for they too were culpable. Therefore, God Himself, YHVH, had to execute the plague. Only God can break His own rules, and He does it sometimes, because His love for us is unconditional.

LOVE IS SEEING

One more vital point of the Exodus story needs elucidation. Just prior to the plague of the firstborn, God required the Israelites to slaughter a lamb and smear its blood on their doorposts so that He would see it as a sign and pass over their homes. Surely God did not need a mark to distinguish the homes of the Israelite slaves from the homes of their Egyptian masters. What then is the meaning of this sign?

Although God's love is unconditional, there is one obstacle that can stand in the way of our receiving His love. God can love us unconditionally, but He can't make us believe that He loves us unconditionally. A poignant passage in the book of Isaiah illustrates this fact. The prophet, in defense of the people of Israel, claimed that they were doing wrong only because God was not present for them. To that, God responded: "I was ready to be sought by those who did not ask for Me. I was ready to be found by those who did not seek Me. I said, 'Here I am, here I am.'"

God is ever-present in our lives and always pours His love upon us, but it is up to us to acknowledge His loving presence—by doing so, we accept His love.

According to some opinions, at the time of the last of the ten plagues, the blood was not smeared on the doorposts facing outside the house, but on the *inside*—not for God to see it but for the Israelites to see it. Obviously, God did not need an identifying sign, but the Israelites needed to tangibly affirm their belief in God's love and His pending gift of freedom. They had to believe in God's unconditional love in order to receive it.

The Talmudic sages taught, "Everything is in the hands of God except awe of God."

The Hebrew word for "awe," *yera*, means both "awe" and "will see." Therefore, everything is in the hands of God except for our willingness to see and be in awe of God. And if we are in awe of God, we will see God. If we are not in awe, if we are not open to seeing God, then God is not seen in our world. It's that simple and that serious.

Some people experience constant divine presence, which means they see and feel God's loving presence, care, and guidance in their lives. They need $800 to pay for a car repair, and an unexpected check for $800 arrives in the mail. They miss a bus, so they get on the next bus, and the person they sit next to turns out to be a friend from twenty years ago.

Why are such experiences not part of everyone's daily life? Because what you see is what you get. To the extent that we believe and acknowledge that God loves us and consistently directs our lives, to that extent we will feel God's love and we will see miracles happen. Each one of us has a choice. We can believe that God created the world, created us, and loves us. Or we can believe that this world is one big accident, a chaotic mess, and we are just dust in the wind, blowing to nowhere. The choice is ours. But we must remember that what we believe is ultimately what we are able to receive and experience in our life.

I was once dating a woman whom I'll call Daphne. I loved Daphne and I wanted to marry her. There was just one thing that bothered me: whenever I paid Daphne a compliment, she dismissed it, and sometimes she even argued that my positive view of her was in error. My gifts were also never received happily: I'd hear "You shouldn't have . . . Why did you waste so much money?" It took me a long time to realize that Daphne simply could not receive my love, as she could not receive my gifts or my compliments. I did everything in my power to show her that I loved her, but Daphne's low self-esteem obstructed her vision. She simply did not believe that anyone could love her. It didn't matter how many times I professed my love to her; she just couldn't *see* my love. So, in a way, it wasn't there for her. As far as she was concerned my love didn't exist.

Everyone is thirsty for love, but how much love we receive is dependent on how much we believe someone could love us. The more we acknowledge and believe in God's unconditional love, the more we see God's love— and God's gifts to us in the form of many miracles—in our life. During the Persian Gulf war of 1991, thirty-nine Scud missiles were launched by Iraq against Israel. Miraculously, only one person died as a direct result of all those missiles falling onto populated areas. It was unbelievable! I remember it well. We would be sitting in our sealed rooms, wearing our gas masks, listening to the reports on the radio. We would hear the Scuds flying overhead. Then a while later, we would hear, "No casualties." I really believed that this was a miracle. Not everyone saw the miracle, though. I remember hearing an interview with the minister of defense. After yet another attack with no casualties, the interviewer asked him, "What do you have to say about this?" The defense minister answered hesitatingly, "I guess another opportunity to tip our hat to Lady Luck." Then, he added haltingly, "Otherwise, I would have to say this is a miracle." I could hear the incredible resistance in his voice; he was trying very hard not to admit the possibility that miracles could happen. But the truth is that if you don't want to believe in miracles, you won't see miracles. If you don't open the door in your mind and heart to that possibility, it will not enter your life.

Traditionally on the night of Passover, as we near the end of reciting the *Haggadah*, we open the door for the prophet Elijah, the harbinger of the Messiah and the final redemption. This seems quite odd. If the soul of Elijah can visit every Seder throughout the world in one night, then surely it can enter without an open door. But we open the door nevertheless, because *we* need to open the door. We need to open our homes and our hearts to Elijah's message of God's eternal love for us.

God tells us, "Nothing can stand in the way of My love for you, except you." Passover is the time to experience and acknowledge God's love. That's why it is the foundation of all the holidays and of all of Judaism. We can't have a relationship with God until we acknowledge that God loves us and will embrace us even when we're not worthy. That's why we read the great love poem, the Song of Songs, on Passover. That's why we spend hours reciting the *Haggadah*, like a lover describing every minute detail of his or her beloved's marriage proposal. We do so because we understand that the more we acknowledge God's love, the more we will experience God's love.

THE REAL MIRACLE

Getting out of Egypt was more than a political emancipation of the nation of Israel. It was a spiritual transformation. The Israelites were not only physically enslaved but also spiritually enmeshed in Egyptian culture. Egypt was the epitome of egotism and haughtiness. Of course, we all know that a person who is egotistical actually lacks self-confidence and true self-esteem. His or her haughty airs are really a cover-up, a compensation for a painful sense of inadequacy. Maimonides, the great twelfth-century philosopher, explains that humanity's lack of self-worth was what led to idolatry. The Egyptians and other ancients were unable to fathom that God would personally care about them. Therefore, they sought help from an intermediate power other than God. They believed that their lives were guided by the stars because God, the Creator, did not personally care about them. They reasoned, "Of what worth are we that the Creator of the world would have any regard for our situation?"

The Passover story teaches us that this attitude is false. In the book of Exodus, God commands, "Don't make intermediate gods for yourselves; keep the Festival of the Matzo." The Talmudic sages explain this odd juxtaposition: "This is to teach us that anyone who disgraces the festival acts as if he is an idolater." In other words, celebrating Passover affirms our belief that God loves us and personally takes care of us; there is no need for any intermediaries between us. To think otherwise is the beginning of idolatry.

God's love and care for us is unconditional, and, therefore, when the Temple stood in Jerusalem, we were obligated to come there and, so to speak, greet God face-to-face. Of course, the presence of God fills the earth and we are in His presence whether we are in Jerusalem or in New York. However, in Jerusalem that truth was (and still is) more readily experienced. On the holiday of Passover even a simpleton could experience a sudden quantum leap in his spiritual level and enjoy a personal loving relationship with God. Each and every one was then able to bask in God's loving presence.

In truth, we are always connected to God. However, three times a year, on the festivals of Passover, Shavuot, and Sukkot, we are able to readily feel that truth. The Torah refers to a festival as a *moed*, which literally means "meeting." The portable sanctuary that the Israelites carried with them in the desert was called the *Ohel Moed*, the Meeting Tent. It was a *place* to meet God. The festivals, however, are a *time* to meet God. The Torah also refers to a festival as a *Mikra Kodesh*, a "calling of holiness," because a festival calls forth from each of us our innate holiness and godliness. Therefore, to deny ourselves the celebration of a *moed*—a direct meeting with God—is akin to accepting the claim of idolatry; it implies that God doesn't love and care about us because we are insignificant and therefore unworthy of His personal attention.

WONDER BREAD

During the seven days of Passover we are required to eat only matzo—unleavened bread that looks somewhat like a cracker and is made of just water and flour. The matzo reminds us that our ancestors were slaves to the Egyptians, who treated them as if they were subhuman and fed them brittle and tasteless bread. It is therefore referred to as the bread of affliction. However, matzo also reminds us of how our ancestors left Egypt in astounding record time, faster than it takes dough to rise. How can matzo symbolize both painful affliction and joyous freedom?

The *Zohar* refers to matzo as the "bread of faith." In other words, when we eat matzo, we are internalizing the message of faith that it embodies. That message is: Know that even if you hit rock bottom and feel far and alienated from God, God is right there to help you and free you from your enslavements, addictions, and obsessions. Even when you've been trapped in your personal Egypt for years and it seems that it will take years to get out, know that, as the Psalmist put it, "the salvation of God is within the blink of an eye."

Although matzo is the bread of affliction and exile, in the blink of an eye it can become the bread of freedom and redemption. Revolutionary transformation is available to us all, as long as we believe it can happen. The paradoxical symbolism of the matzo teaches us that God Himself, at any moment, can create a miracle. Even if we reach the bottom, we should never despair or give up. Matzo, the bread of faith, is an antidote to despair and nurtures within us faith and hope.

The Exodus from Egypt assures us that if the Israelites could get out of Egypt, then we too can get out of any situation. Certainly God could have orchestrated the Israelites' liberation differently: He could have arranged for them to earn their freedom through some worthy deed. However, He did precisely the opposite. He brought them out without merit so as to instill forever within us the confidence that His love is unconditional. Therefore, no matter how low any of us may fall, we should never despair. The paradoxical symbolism of the matzo also teaches us that in the very bitterness of affliction and exile lies the sweetness of freedom and redemption. The great Hasidic master Rabbi Nachman of Breslav taught, "Being far from God itself is for the purpose of coming close . . . the downfall can be transformed into a great ascent." It all depends on the way you look at it. The matzo is basically tasteless, but if you choose to, you can taste the freedom and redemption that lie at the core of affliction and exile.

Perhaps this is the meaning of God's response to Abraham when he requested a sign that the land of Israel would be an eternal inheritance for him and his descendants. God showed him the future history of exile. At that moment, Abraham experienced great fear. But God comforted him, saying, "Know that your offspring will be strangers in a strange land. There, they will be enslaved and afflicted for four hundred years. [But] also the nation that will afflict them I will judge, and your children will leave with great wealth." In other words, although your offspring will endure much suffering, they will survive and even profit from it.

So don't worry; don't lose faith. Even the darkest hours are the very seeds of growth, transformation, renewal, and redemption. Rav Nachman of Breslav also taught, "Sometimes when you want to come close to God, you encounter new and even greater obstacles than before. However, don't let that discourage you. God is only challenging you, so you will try even harder and thereby come even closer. It's really all for the best." The Sfat Emes, another great Hasidic master, taught that on Passover we can achieve a huge leap forward in our spiritual evolution. In other words, although in general, great feats take much time, on Passover we can move at a pace that transcends the limitations of time.

The Hebrew word for Egypt is *Mitzraim*, which also translates as "narrowness." Indeed, Egypt represented the deification of the narrow confines and limitations of nature, time, and space. To leave Egypt also meant to leave this narrow and confining attitude. It meant leaving the world of nature, governed by physical laws and subject to logic based on what only the physical senses can perceive, in order to cross over into a new spiritual worldview—the world without limitations, the world of unconditional love.

HAPPY BIRTHDAY

Passover is the birthday of the nation of Israel—the time when the Jewish people became a nation. It is a time to remember that we are all children of God, born with an innate godliness. Indeed, our relationship to God is similar to that of a child to a parent.

The Torah refers to the people of Israel as the "first-born child" of God. This is because they were the first nation in history to believe that God is like a loving parent and they are His beloved children. And that His love is unconditional and forever.

May everyone in the world realize that they, too, are the beloved children of God.

—TWO—

Shavuot

Celebrating Responsibility and Freedom

After the miraculous Exodus from Egypt, the Israelites traveled in the desert for seven weeks until they reached Mount Sinai on the sixth day of the Hebrew month of Sivan. There they experienced an unprecedented encounter with God. They heard the voice of God and received the Torah and its commandments—the mitzvot. Whereas Passover is the time when the Jewish people became a nation, Shavuot (the Festival of Weeks) is a time to celebrate the mitzvot—the responsibilities implicit in the loving relationship we are meant to enjoy with God. This holiday can be likened to the bar mitzvah.

I recall my own bar mitzvah. Unfortunately, because I was not aware of its real meaning, my bar mitzvah was more bar than mitzvah. It was just a big drinking party with my friends, not an event celebrating the acceptance of my responsibilities as a Jew.

My bar mitzvah speech was also a farce. I spent months writing it, because I knew it could mean big money. If you say the right thing, who knows what kinds of checks people will write at the end of it! I spent night after night trying to figure out how to introduce the whole thing with a funny joke or attention-grabbing story.

Finally, it hit me. I remembered a word from Hebrew school: *bakhur*. I was called a "bar mitzvah *bakhur*," which means "bar mitzvah lad." I could not wait to tell my mother how I was going to introduce my bar mitzvah speech.

"Listen to this," I said to her. "I'm going to stand up and say, 'Today, I am a bar mitzvah banker . . . err . . . I mean *bakhur*.'" I thought it was a very funny (even if staged) slip of the tongue.

My mother looked at me and said, "You're not saying that."

"What do you mean? It's hysterical!" I said. "It's going to make me a lot of money. 'Today I am a bar mitzvah banker . . . I mean *bakhur*.' It's great!"

But my mother stood firm and I ended up saying, "Today I am a man, and I will accept all my responsibilities and be a good Jew"—exactly what everybody else says. And it meant to me what it means to most people today: nothing.

Recently a friend asked me if I would meet with his son, Sam, and help him prepare his bar mitzvah speech. I generally don't teach thirteen-year-olds, but for a friend I made an exception. I met with Sam and began to share with him some insights into the section of the Torah (known as the weekly portion) that he would be reading in the synagogue. He was listening attentively, nodding his head every so often, so I talked and talked. I even started to explain to him some of the mystical meanings behind the passages he would be reading. I was very impressed that he seemed to be really understanding me. After about an hour of my monologue, I finally asked him, "Sammy, do you have any questions?"

He said, "Yeah, just one. Why do I have to obey all these commandments, keep all these rules?"

Well, I felt pretty silly. Here I was going off the deep end when he didn't even know what his bar mitzvah meant.

I asked him, "Sammy, do you like football?"

"I love it! I play it all the time."

"Do you know the rules?" I continued.

"Of course. You can't play if you don't know the rules."

"Why not?"

" 'Cuz then there would be no game. You couldn't win or lose. There'd be no touchdowns, no out of bounds, no violations, no penalties. Without the rules it would just be chaos and no fun."

"Precisely. And that's true about the game of life also. Without rules and regulations it would be chaos, no fun, no adventure, no challenge. You couldn't win or lose. And even though we all know 'It's not whether you win or lose but how you play the game,' without rules there is no way to evaluate 'how you play the game.' The Torah's commandments are the game rules of life, and God is the referee."

In the end, Sammy got psyched for his bar mitzvah.

On Shavuot we celebrate the day when we become players in the game of life, because on this day, God gave us the rules.

Without rules, there is no game. You can't even play a game of football without rules, let alone live a life! If there is no right and wrong, then what difference does it make what you do? If there is nothing to violate, there is nothing to fulfill. Without the Torah's game rules for living, the world is just one big mess and your choices are meaningless.

The Torah, however, is much more than the rules of life. Torah is a living encounter with God. The revelation of God at Mount Sinai wasn't simply an opportunity for the Israelites to receive God's laws but to experience God's love. What happened at Mount Sinai was a personal encounter with the divine power. It wasn't just God handing down laws; it was God allowing Himself to be known, to be felt. What happened at Mount Sinai was an ecstatic experience—the newly freed slaves meeting God in the most intimate encounter ever recorded.

The experience at Mount Sinai was not only a revelation of God's truth; more important, it was a revelation of God's love. Torah was, and continues to be, God's love letter to His children. It is the greatest gift ever received, because it embodies God's presence.

When you learn the Torah, you can actually feel God's closeness to you. The Talmud teaches that when God gave the Torah to the Israelites, He said, "I am giving you My soul in writing."

Imagine that one day you receive a love letter. You are at work and eating lunch in the employee cafeteria, and someone drops a letter in front of you. You immediately see that it's a letter from the one you love. Do you rip open the envelope and start to speed-read through the letter? No, of course you don't. You save this letter. You're going to read it in a very special place, because this letter deserves every ounce of your attention.

Now imagine you're in that special place. You open the letter carefully, you start to read your beloved's words, and you actually begin to hear your beloved's voice. And then you feel your beloved's presence.

If you're anything like me, you'll read the letter over and over again, because you know there's much more to this letter. The first time you read it, you get the simple meaning. But then you read it even more carefully. You notice that she tells you about the weather, and then she starts talking about her mother. What's the connection, you wonder. You then read the letter again, and now you see that there are hints in this letter. You pay attention not only to what she says but also to the way she has structured her sentences. Then you go over it again, because you realize that it's even deeper than that. You even look at how she forms the letters. There are secrets in the nuances of the actual shape of her letters!

Once you've analyzed every aspect of your beloved's message, you carefully refold the letter, place it in its envelope, and tuck it away for safekeeping. You save this letter because you sense the presence of your beloved in these few sheets of paper.

Now let's imagine that someone else is reading that letter. Is that person going to feel the presence of your beloved? No. They will just read the letter's simple meaning and extract the pertinent information. But for you, it's different. You can't just read the letter; you must be involved in it. And through your involvement with the words, nuances, and deeper meanings, you meet your beloved.

This, in essence, is the experience of learning Torah. Through our involvement with the text, we hear God's voice, feel the divine presence, experience God's love, and relive the revelation at Sinai each day of our lives. Therefore, the Torah embodies not only a way of life but also a way to love. The wisdom and commandants of the Torah empower us to love each other and to love God. Shavuot is a day to celebrate the laws but also to celebrate the love in the law. But that's not all. The Torah is even deeper than that.

A MISSION FROM GOD

I will share with you a very strange story from the Talmud. The sages encoded deep ideas into such strange stories. This one conveys a profound truth about who we are, what the Torah is, and why God gave it to us.

When Moses ascended to heaven to receive the Torah, the ministering angels said to the Holy One, "Sovereign of the universe, what is one born of a woman doing among us (who were born of God)?" In other words, what is this imperfect creature doing up here with us perfect beings? How could a mortal ascend to the level of angels?

"He's not staying," responded God. "He just came to pick up something—the Torah."

The angels were even more upset. "What? Are You about to give this frail human that cherished treasure that You have held on to for 974 generations before the world was created? What is this mortal man that you care about him? Isn't Your name already sufficiently exalted on the earth?"

By saying, "Isn't Your name already sufficiently exalted on the earth?" the angels were cynically reminding God that human beings have consistently desecrated God's name through all their wrongdoings. They were saying, "How can You give human beings your holy Torah? Keep it in heaven. Give it to us!"

Before I continue with the story, I have to point out that the sages are teaching us here that the Torah is more than the game rules of life and more than a love letter from God. It contains an *assignment* from God, a *mission* from God to be performed on God's behalf. That's why Moses, in order to get the Torah, had to ascend to the angelic realm.

An angel is an agent of God, a godly ambassador

appointed to perform a divine mission. But we humans also have the opportunity to perform a mission on behalf of God. To accept the Torah means to accept a divine mission. By so doing, we become God's agents. According to Jewish law, someone whom you appoint to be your agent is equipotent to yourself. You have given this person your power of attorney, to act on your behalf. This is the amazing power, responsibility, and privilege entrusted to us through the Torah. This is also the purpose of the commandments. They are directives from God, statements defining the mission to be performed on God's behalf by human beings on earth. When you accept the mission of the commandments, you become God's agent on earth, just as angels are God's agents in heaven.

According to the Talmudic story, the angels didn't know the details of this mission, but they knew that it was really important to God, since He had been holding on to it for so long and had not appointed anyone to carry it out. But to appoint a human being? That was absurd!

In response to the angels' complaints, God said to Moses, "Tell them. Explain to them why you deserve this mission. Explain to them your qualifications."

Most people think that the Torah is about believing in God. But that's only half the story. The Torah is also about believing in yourself. To accept the Torah, you must have a tremendous amount of self-esteem. You must believe that you are worthy to be God's agent on earth and that you were sent here to fulfill a sacred mission.

The message of Shavuot is: You are important and significant to God. You have been given the opportunity to represent the Almighty. You can represent God, because you have been entrusted with His power of attorney to act on His behalf. This view is at odds with the Greek view of religion that has dominated Western culture. The Greeks believed that the gods were so great that it was beneath their dignity to bother with humans. But here God offers a mission to Moses. However, he says, "Unless you realize for yourself what your qualifications are, you can't be entrusted with the mission."

Moses then grabs hold of God's throne and is empowered with an amazing confidence to face the angels. In their presence, he asks God, "What's in Your Torah?"

God answers, "I am the Lord your God, who brought you out of Egypt." Moses then challenges the angels: "Did you go to Egypt and serve Pharaoh? What relevance is the Torah to you?" In other words, Moses argues, "Were you slaves, oppressed by the Egyptians for 210 years?"

The angels concede. They were not. They have lived only a perfect, blissful life in heaven.

Moses continues to make his case. "God, what else is written in Your Torah?"

"You shall not have other gods."

Moses confronts the angels: "Are you living among nations who worship idols?" The angels say, "Nahh, we're angels!"

Moses continues, "God, what else is in the Torah?"

"Keep the Shabbat. Honor your father and mother. Don't murder. Don't commit adultery. Don't steal."

"Angels," Moses challenges, "do you work hard? Do you need rest? Do you have fathers and mothers whom you have to honor? Does jealousy exist among you? Do you have an evil inclination?"

These were the qualifications that Moses presented to merit the mission of Torah for humankind. We humans are lowly beings; we are attacked by evil urges all the time. We live in a materialistic society filled with daily seductions. That's why we should get the Torah! We qualify for this mission because we make so many mistakes. We are conflicted beings inundated with problems and challenges from within and without. *We are perfect for this job, because we are so imperfect!* So the next time you call us "born of a woman," say it with respect.

The angels were impressed with this argument, and they acquiesced. The story ends with their words of praise, "Holy One, blessed be He! Oh Lord, how excellent is your name in all the earth!"

FOR GOODNESS' SAKE

What is the mission of Torah? What can we frail earthlings do for omnipotent God? The answer is: We can embrace the challenges of life, overcome evil, and choose goodness.

God is good, was good, and always will be good. Therefore, can God *choose* goodness?

I know a fellow who has dozens of guests at his home every weekend, in keeping with the commandment to welcome strangers. When I complimented him on his hospitality, he said, "What are you talking about? It comes naturally to me. It's not a struggle for me. I love to do this!"

Is he really choosing goodness? If it comes naturally, is it complete goodness? Goodness that isn't chosen is not the greatest good. Only after you struggle with evil and choose goodness will you accomplish true and complete goodness.

If God is only good, does God struggle with evil? Can God experience complete goodness through overcoming evil and choosing the good?

Yes, through you and me.

God created us and appoints us to be His agents—to act on His behalf. God therefore participates in complete goodness through our choices. This is our service to God: to choose goodness. That's why we're in a world so full of allurements to do evil: so that we can rise to the challenge and choose the good.

We are highly qualified for this mission because we have an evil inclination that challenges us daily. And we live in a world that presents constant allurements and seductions. We are able to fail but also to succeed. We are able to destroy but also to build. We are able to choose to do great evil but also to choose to do amazing good. Angels are perfect; they have no evil inclination. They have no free choice. They can't struggle. They can't fail. They cannot choose goodness.

The Talmud teaches that you don't ultimately succeed until you have first failed. In other words, part of fulfilling the divine mission is to fail, regret the failure, resolve to change, choose goodness, and succeed. In fact, sometimes God orchestrates a situation for us to fail so that we can get to an even higher place once we fix our mistake.

The book of Ecclesiastes teaches, "There's no holy person in the world that doesn't transgress."

To err is human.

Note that Ecclesiastes specifies "in the world," because if you managed to get out of this world, you could be perfect. If you lived on some deserted island completely removed from society, then you would never hurt anyone's feelings, you would never get into an argument, and you would never get jealous and possibly never make a mistake.

But you don't live on a deserted island, and you can't completely remove yourself from society—though people try.

Our divine mission—if we're willing to accept it—is to be human, embrace the challenges of life on earth, and choose goodness. This is how we serve God. Angels sing God's praises in a perfect, heavenly world. However, human praises surpass angels' praises, because we praise God from earth, soiled with imperfections, problems, and challenges. This is our greatness.

God does not expect us to be perfect. In fact, if we were perfect, we could not have qualified for the mission of Torah. We imperfect humans are the perfect candidates for the job.

When the angels understood this, they gave Moses gifts—useful secrets. They wanted to invest in the human enterprise. They wanted to be shareholders in Human

Goodness, Inc. They reasoned that if they couldn't work for the company, they could at least invest in it and enjoy dividends as shareholders.

God is the major investor in Human Goodness, Inc. God invested a spark of His Divine Self in human beings in order to participate in this world. This is the meaning of the mystical tradition that teaches that God desires to be in this world. God lives and participates in this world through you and me—if we accept the mission. This is the real meaning of God creating humanity in His image.

Every human being has the potential to be an agent for God. Everything we do can be for God's sake. This is the greatest honor and pleasure a person can experience. To live for ourselves is no great honor, but to live for God, to choose goodness for God's sake—this is heaven on earth. On Shavuot we celebrate having a divine mission on earth.

WHAT HAPPENED AT SINAI?

When God spoke at Mount Sinai, He opened with: "*I, YHVH, am your God, who took you out of Egypt.*" As mentioned in the previous chapter, the Israelites endured 210 years of cruel oppression under the tyranny of the Pharaoh before being freed from slavery by a series of miracles. They crossed the Red Sea and received the commandments at Mount Sinai only fifty days after leaving Egypt, so there is no possible way they could have forgotten what had just happened. Why then does God begin by reminding them of this fact? How are we to understand this strange statement?

Imagine that six weeks ago you almost drowned and a stranger by the name of Jack came out of nowhere and saved your life. You owe him everything. You intend to name all your future children after him: Jack, Jacqueline, Jacket, Jacuzzi. . . . And then the phone rings, and the voice you will never ever forget says to you, "Hi, this is Jack, you know, Jack who saved your life." Does he really need to remind you who he is? As far as you are concerned, is there even another Jack in the world?

Similarly, God's statement—which is the very first of the Ten Commandments—seems just as bizarre. It doesn't even seem to be a commandment.

In fact, this statement commands us to know that God is the "I"—the Great "I"—who is the source of our freedom. And just as the miraculous Exodus from Egypt expressed His unconditional love for us, so too the commandments express His unconditional love for us. And if we fail to uphold them sometimes, we need not worry. God is always on our side.

The mistake many people make is to think of God's commands as demands. They are not.

A demand implies a threat, but a command is, in fact, an invitation to commune, to work with, and to work for, God. God's mitzvot are empowering. They give our lives meaning. Through the mitzvot, we transcend our ego and petty concerns, pattern our earthly lives according to a heavenly order, and bond ourselves with the Great "I."

The Torah tells us that before the Israelites even knew what the mitzvot were, they accepted them unequivocally and unconditionally, telling God, "We will do and we will hear."

The Talmud says that God responded in admiration: "'Who revealed this secret to My children—the secret that the ministering angels use for themselves?' As it says in the Psalms, 'Bless God, you angels of His, you mighty ones who perform His bidding, hearkening to the voice of His word.'"

The Talmud also tells us that a heretic criticized the Israelites for being so impetuous and putting their mouth before their ears. It would have made more sense to first hear what the commandments would be and then decide whether or not to accept them. So what did the Israelites understand that this heretic obviously was missing?

The heretic saw God as a being separate from His creation, and therefore he saw the mitzvot as God's demands and their acceptance as an act of self-sacrifice. As far as he was concerned, the Israelites were surrendering their will and their self-interests to the will and self-interest of this other being—God. But the Israelites knew better. They knew that because God is their Greater Self, there couldn't be any conflict of interest, because the self—the soul—is a spark of the Great Self, God.

To live according to the mitzvot is not self-sacrifice; it is actually an empowering act of even greater self-expression. In sync with God, doing the will of God, I am even more myself. This is the secret of the angels.

The Talmud teaches that there is no greater joy than

doing a mitzvah. Yet I know so many people who think that living a life according to the Torah's commandments means giving up the pleasures of this world for the eternal rewards of the next world. They think of mitzvot as simply good deeds. Like brownie points, you rack them up, you save them, and you cash them in in the next world.

But in actuality the true reward reaped from the commandments is that we become holy. The prophet Isaiah teaches that God is "holy, holy, holy . . . His splendor fills the entire earth." God's holiness is so beyond this world ("holy, holy, holy") that God can simultaneously be in it ("His splendor fills the entire earth"). A holy person is not someone who, by staying away from the world, is able to be above it. Rather, a holy person feels no conflict at all with the physical world. A holy person can be above it and totally in it at the same time. A holy person can be in the middle of a traffic jam and still be above it, riding along with peace of mind, without becoming aggravated. A holy person can enjoy the physical pleasures of this world without becoming addicted to or enslaved by them. This is because holiness encompasses both transcendence and immanence at the same time. When we serve God and work on His behalf, we become like God—beyond, and yet within, this finite and temporal world.

But I must warn you that the mitzvot can be a form of slavery if they are not practiced with the right intentions. The Talmud says that a person can follow all the commandments to the letter and still be "ugly." Issuing an even stronger warning, the Talmud also says that, although the Torah is an elixir of life, it can also become deadly poison.

How so?

Depending on our attitude toward it, Torah can be an incredible journey of the soul or just another ego trip. If, for example, we seek to fulfill the Torah's commandments in order to please another human being whom we fear or want to impress, then we are engaging in a form of idol worship.

Unfortunately, this happens too often. For some people, fulfilling the commandments to the letter is a goal unto itself and is not really connected to any desire to lovingly serve God and bond with Him. For them, the mitzvot have become idols.

Slipping into idolatry is easier than it may seem. When Moses went up the mountain to receive the Ten Commandments written in stone by God, the Israelites impatiently waited below. When he did not return when they expected, they panicked and built the Golden Calf. A few hours later, Moses came down from Mount Sinai holding the two tablets of stone, and he was shocked to see how quickly the Israelites had lost the clarity of "We will do and we will listen" and deteriorated into the idolatrous ways of Egypt. He was especially devastated by the sight of them rejoicing around an idol. It's one thing to make a mistake in a moment of despair, but it's another to be happy about it. At this disgusting sight, Moses threw down the tablets and broke them. The Jewish oral tradition says that when the elders of Israel saw what Moses was about to do, they tried to grab the tablets from him. But he was stronger than they, and the tablets shattered. The Talmud, surprisingly, says that God congratulated him for breaking the tablets.

Moses was a master educator. He realized that the Israelites were really not ready for the Torah. Had they really understood what they were about to receive, they would have never made the Golden Calf and certainly would not have rejoiced over it. So Moses feared that they would simply make the Torah into another idol. They had obviously lost the critical prerequisite for truly receiving the Torah—the desire to serve God and bond with Him. Without that intention, even the mitzvot would become a form of idolatry for them—not a means to a loving relationship with God but an end in itself.

A joke describes Moses coming down from Mount Sinai with the tablets of the Ten Commandments. "I've got good news and bad news," he announces. "The good news is that I got Him down to ten . . . The bad news is that adultery is still in."

This joke illustrates a common attitude. People think that the commandments spoil the fun in life. God—like a domineering taskmaster—wants to bring us down to our knees, praying all day, being somber, sad, quiet. In other words, there is a conflict of interest between us and God.

People think that doing what God wants is oppressive. Serving God implies a slave-master relationship. But that is not what serving God really means. The opportunity to serve God is the greatest gift we could ever imagine. It's empowering! Serving God means that we can do something *for* God. Far from being oppressive—it's an incredible honor!

Working for God is not a diminishing experience. It's the most incredible elevation of status. If I seek to build my business for my sake, to make money for *me*, it is really no big deal. But if I seek to build my business in order to promote God's purpose in this world, to bring into the world more love, peace, kindness, justice, wisdom, to be an instrument revealing divine qualities and ideals in the world, then I tap into unbelievable joy and opportunity! This is the secret to living a profoundly meaningful and fulfilling life. And this is what was revealed at Sinai.

REVELING IN THE REVELATION

Revelation is God-given knowledge meant to guide us in our world. It begins where the empirical knowledge of humanity ends. Empirical knowledge can take us only to the outer limits of our own perspective, but revelation takes us beyond those limits.

This is why the commandments can never make complete sense from a human perspective, because the very definition of revelation is knowledge bestowed from a divine perspective.

Revelation is like the traffic station on the radio. You are driving down Route 83, and you wonder which is the quickest way to your destination. Is there a traffic jam ahead? Should you get off at the next exit and take an alternate route? Or take your chances with the traffic lights on the main thoroughfare? There is really no way for you to know; you cannot possibly see the next two miles of roadway. But the traffic helicopter hovering overhead sees everything. From its perspective, all the highways and traffic patterns are perfectly visible. So you tune in to the traffic station, and you hear the clear message: "Traffic jam on Route 83 between Kilmer and Havington. If you're traveling north, exit at Route 144." Even the most deluxe, state-of-the-art automobile can never know what the helicopter knows, unless the helicopter communicates to it. That is revelation.

Although revelation is information given to human beings from a higher perspective, the content of the revelation is still expressed in human terminology. Thus, when the Israelites experienced God directly at the splitting of the Red Sea, they perceived Him as a warrior. At the revelation at Sinai, they experienced God as a wise sage. The prophet Ezekiel had a vision and saw the celestial chariot and throne. What is all this about? Had they made the mistake of perceiving God as an object?

Not at all. Prophetic revelation comes in the form of transcendental messages, which the human mind translates into images. Have you ever listened to a symphony while lying on the couch with your eyes closed? Sometimes as you listen to the music, images flash through your mind. A certain airy flute section may conjure up the image of a butterfly. Turbulent sounds may evoke a storm. Although your mind is translating the sounds into pictures, you know that neither the butterfly nor the storm is an actual picture of the sounds you are hearing.

So too in revelation, the prophetic experience is trans-lated into an image, but the image is no more a picture of God than the butterfly is a picture of those musical sounds.

During the revelation at Mount Sinai, all the Israelites became prophets, and they understood creation and its purpose in an instant. This is why they accepted the Torah and its principles without hesitation (even if they acted as if they had second thoughts later).

A MATTER OF PRINCIPLES

The Torah states, "It was the sixth day, and God com-pleted the heavens and earth." In describing the first through the fifth days of creation, the Torah leaves out the article *the*. But here it is specific: "*the* sixth day."

The Talmud teaches that "*the* sixth day" hints at the sixth day of the Hebrew month of Sivan when the chil-dren of Israel received the Torah from God at Mount Sinai. It continues to explain that God made a deal with the universe: If the Israelites accept the Torah on the sixth day of Sivan, then the universe will continue to exist. If the Israelites do not accept the Torah, then the world will return to its original state of chaos and form-lessness. So we see that, according to Judaism, the Torah is much more cosmic than simple rituals and ethical laws would imply.

The Midrash, which is part of the Jewish oral tradi-tion, metaphorically describes the Torah as saying about itself with pride, "God looked at me and created the world. Through me, the world was created." What the Midrash means is that God also follows the universal laws of the Torah and that He created the world according to its principles. The Torah is more than what it appears to be. Not only is it the game rules of life, a love letter from God, and a mission from God, it is also the science of God.

Imagine that, once upon a time, a fellow was sitting under an apple tree when an apple fell on his head. "Isn't that strange," he said, surprised, "apples fall!" He had never really given the phenomenon much attention.

"What about my pencil? What about my book?" he wondered, as he picked them up and let them go.

"Aha! Apples, books, and pencils fall! There seems to be a consistent force that draws things down," he realized.

Did he invent gravity? No, he just *discovered* it. Gravity is a physical principle that has been guiding the movement of physical bodies since the beginning of time. Having finally understood it, this fellow was able to articulate a principle that had always been the force through which God directs the world. This is what Sir Isaac Newton did when he formulated his theory of gravitation. This is, in fact, what all scientists attempt to do. Albert Einstein formulated his unified field theory because he believed there must be a consistent set of principles that govern the movement of life.

We naturally live in accordance with the laws of gravity. It is obvious to us all that it would be absurd for us to oppose it. However, what if a group of activists were to decide that they have had it with gravity and organize a world movement of antigravitationists: "Who says we must abide by gravity? It's archaic and oppressive. We are going to establish a new world order. We shall overcome!"

Next thing you know, thousands of people are signing petitions, declaring their opposition to gravity. They convince millions that gravity is a plot fabricated by scientists. "It's a downer!" they protest. Then they hold a mass antigravitation rally on a mountaintop. "Down with gravity, up with people!"

The rally climaxes as the leader declares, "This is it! Let's race off the cliff and show the world!" They charge full speed ahead and leap off the cliff, singing, "Dowwwwwn with gravityyyyy, dowwwwwn with gravityyyyy." And they fall to their deaths.

Whether you accept gravity does not make a difference to its existence and its influence upon you; it does not ask your opinion. As long as the earth exists, gravity is a principle that was, is, and will be. To deny it only brings ruin.

THE LAWS OF HUMAN NATURE

If there are physical principles that govern our existence, perhaps there are also spiritual or ethical principles. And just maybe, as definitive as the laws of gravity are, there are ethical and spiritual laws equally definitive.

Are ethics a matter of consensus or social contract, or are ethics established laws of the universe? Does the majority rule in all matters? Is wanton cruelty merely a matter not to our taste, or is it absolutely wrong?

Judaism teaches that the spiritual/moral dimension of life is no different from the physical dimension. And, just as gravity and other laws of nature govern physical life, there are spiritual laws that govern spiritual life. And these laws have been guiding the universe since its very inception.

God, so to speak, looked in the Torah and created the world according to the principles and laws set forth therein. Adam and Eve were originally in sync with the flow of life. They intuited the universal laws of the Torah, but the snake confused them, and they lost their natural connection to God and His law. During the time of Noah, there was a possibility for a mass revelation of the Torah's eternal laws, but the generation was not ready or willing, so that generation perished in the Flood. Then came Abraham, an individual so attuned to his soul and the inner core of his being that he intuitively followed the details of Torah law.

When, 1,500 years later, the entire people of Israel were positioned for a revelation of the Torah, they already knew what the Torah contained subconsciously. This is because we all know the Torah subconsciously—it is encoded in all our souls, but we forget it as soon as we are born. Only rare individuals like Abraham manage to remember it and to align their lives to it.

Therefore, what was revealed at Mount Sinai was nothing new. The laws of the Torah revealed the divine principles and laws that had always directed life. The experience at Mount Sinai—which we celebrate on Shavuot—was a revelation of the universal principles of spirituality and ethics. The laws of the Torah had been there all along, but it was only then that the descendants of Abraham were ready and willing to receive them.

If some of these moral principles seem obvious to us today, it is because, since they were received at Mount Sinai, they have permeated the consciousness of the world, as the Irish Catholic author Thomas Cahill has documented in his best-selling book *The Gifts of the Jews*, and as the Christian historian Paul Johnson has outlined in his definitive work *The History of the Jews*. Johnson writes:

> All the great conceptual discoveries of the human intellect seem obvious and inescapable once they have been revealed, but require a special genius to formulate them for the first time. The Jews had this gift [the Torah]. To them we owe the idea of equality before the law, both divine and human; of the sanctity of life and the dignity of human person; of the individual conscience and so a personal redemption; of collective conscience and so of social responsibility; of peace as an abstract ideal and love as the foundation of justice, and many other items which constitute the basic moral furniture of the human mind. Without the Jews it might have been a much emptier place. . . . It is almost beyond our capacity to

imagine how the world would have fared if they
had never emerged.

It is almost beyond our capacity to imagine how the world would have fared if they had not received the Torah at Mount Sinai.

The Torah embodies the universal principles and laws of moral order. Social contract has no influence over it. If we try to transgress its principles, we damage ourselves and the universe. It is only to our benefit to recognize these principles and laws and to live in accordance with them. To do otherwise is to be as foolish as an antigravitationist and to end up the same way (spiritually speaking).

To choose to follow the Torah and abide by these principles is to choose a life of freedom. What people do not realize is that living in tandem with the very forces that guide the world frees us from having to struggle against them. Living in opposition to them causes stress and disease.

When God offered the Torah to the Israelites, they recognized that God was presenting the principles upon which life had been functioning since its very inception. Their first response was, "We will do it." They did not try to figure out whether the Torah fit their values, nor did they expect God to conform to their standards. Rather, they wanted to conform to God's standards. In so doing, they experienced the ultimate pleasure—the reward—of living in harmony with divine ideals. They did not feel as if the Torah was imposed from without. Rather, they felt that the Torah was exposed from within. They understood that the Torah was, is, and always will be the guiding force of the universe, because it is at the core of all being.

In the Garden of Eden, the snake convinced Adam and Eve that conforming to God's will and obeying His command are self-diminishing. The snake's message was: "Do your own thing, be your own god. You can set your own standards for what is good and bad. You do not have to subordinate yourself by accepting the rules of God."

But the Israelites understood that the Torah is not self-diminishing; it is self-fulfilling. This is why they accepted the Torah without questioning. After all, is it self-diminishing to accord yourself to the force of gravity? On the contrary, it is lifesaving to know and to adhere to the laws of gravity. By knowing this universal physical principle, you can design a rocket to travel into outer space and perhaps discover new worlds. Similarly, knowing the laws of the spiritual universe enables you to connect with the guiding forces of life. That is the spiritual definition of freedom.

When the Israelites left Egypt, they experienced freedom from oppression by a human ruler, the Pharaoh. However, when they received the Torah at Mount Sinai on the sixth of Sivan, they reached a new level of freedom—the freedom to be themselves.

On Shavuot we celebrate our responsibility and our freedom to live in accordance with our essence, to actualize our potential, to be a player in history, to be a lover of God, to be a servant and an agent of God, to work on His behalf and live in joyous harmony with the universe.

What a day! Happy bar mitzvah!

—THREE—

Tisha B'Av

Celebrating Loss
and Sadness

On Tisha B'Av, the ninth day of the Hebrew month of Av (which occurs generally in August), we mourn the loss of the Holy Temple—*Beit HaMikdash* in Hebrew—that once stood in Jerusalem. On this day the Babylonians destroyed the First Temple (built by Solomon) in 586 B.C.E., and the Romans demolished the Second (rebuilt) Temple in 70 C.E.

Each Tisha B'Av we have a custom to read *Eicha*, or the book of Lamentations, a painful account of the prophet Jeremiah's intense sorrow over the destruction. In addition to reading *Eicha*, we abstain from any physical pleasures the entire day. We are not allowed to eat, drink, wash our bodies for enjoyment, or wear leather shoes, and we sit on the ground rather than in chairs. We are also not allowed to say hello to each other.

This last prohibition is perhaps the most difficult for me and yet the most meaningful. In Jerusalem in the summertime, when there are many new faces to meet and old friends to greet, not saying hello to people saddens me deeply. If only we felt the simple pain of not saying hello to each other and internalized the meaning of this mournful act, perhaps we would then be more careful to warmly and lovingly greet each other and not hurt each other.

But, without a Temple, we are out of touch with the presence of God within the world and within each other. This is the real tragedy and the real reason we mourn. The more we understand this spiritual loss, the more we appreciate the enormous significance of the Temple and the intense pain of living without it. On Tisha B'Av we celebrate this pain by transforming it into spiritual cravings and yearnings for the restoration of the Temple and everything it stands for.

A LOOK AT PAIN

This past Tisha B'Av, I watched my thirteen-year-old son publicly recite *Eicha* for the first time. As he read Jeremiah's heart-wrenching words, his voice started to quiver and tears began to pour down his cheeks. I thought to myself, "What am I doing to my son? Why put him through this pain and cause him such grief? Why pass on to him a history of such pain?" I too began to cry.

Growing up the son of a Holocaust survivor, I was very conscious of the pain of being Jewish. My mother's experiences in the Holocaust made me aware of the horrors that Jews have experienced throughout history. Until I revisited Judaism in my teens, I did not love being Jewish. In fact, I hated it. I realized that if I had been born a couple of decades earlier, I too would have known the horrors of life in a concentration camp.

I grew up in a non-Jewish community, where I was one of only two Jews in my school. I was often harassed because I was Jewish. When I worked hard in school and got high marks, the kids called me a brownnoser. When I did not attend school during Jewish holidays, I was called a lazy Jew.

Focused on the pain of my Jewish identity, it took me years to find within it power and joy. But I did, when I realized that it is necessary for us humans to feel pain in order to feel joy.

JOY AND PAIN: THE DANCE OF LIFE

As counterintuitive as it may seem, there is no joy without sadness. We strive to be happy our whole lives and to avoid all sadness and pain. But only people who truly know pain and sadness can truly know pleasure and joy. And only people who truly know pleasure and joy can know pain and sadness. We live in a dualistic world. To be fully alive and aware, we must be willing to embrace the total spectrum of human emotions and experience. At the very breathtaking peaks of life are the beginnings of the slopes down. The mountains and the valleys are connected and one.

Although God promised that eventually the Temple will be rebuilt, the Jewish tradition teaches that only those who truly understand and feel the pain over the destruction of the Temple will have the ability to rejoice at the rebuilding of the Temple. In a strange way, on Tisha B'Av, we take pleasure in our ability to mourn, and we experience profound fulfillment in our tears.

Unfortunately, society has perpetuated the silly attitude that men should not cry. But without a good cry, we cannot have a good laugh. One of the most powerful and beautiful moments of my life was when I cried for the first time in front of my wife. In fact, crying in front of your spouse is one of the greatest opportunities to share your genuine humanness. Animals do not cry, nor do they laugh. The laughing hyena is not expressing intense joy; it is simply making a sound that sounds to us like laughter. According to the Kabbalah, animals feel pain, but it's not as if in the middle of their pain they think, "Oy, if only I could be happy."

Human beings, however, are able to remember the joyous moments of their lives, even when they are in pain. And in their most joyous moments, they are able to remember their pain.

Some years ago I attended the wedding of a widower with eight children. His first wife, a young woman, had suffered from cancer for several years before finally succumbing to it. He badly needed a wife after all the years of illness and stress, and his children needed a mother, so he remarried quickly. At the wedding mixed emotions were apparent. While relatives and friends were happy for him, they still remembered his first wife and were poignantly aware of her passing. They cried as they wished him and his new wife *"Mazel Tov!"*

Such paradoxical experiences capture the profundity of life and the unique power of human consciousness.

Illustrating this point, the prophet Jeremiah, in the very midst of his lamentations, says, "What does a living human being have to complain about?" It is a serious question. Are we complaining about our crying and suffering? Are we complaining about complaining? Jeremiah realizes in the depth of his pain that we cannot know the joy of being alive without experiencing the pain that comes with it, and that we should be thankful for the very ability to cry, since it is a sign that we are fully alive and conscious. Our ability to cry and feel pain is itself part of our ability to laugh and feel pleasure. Together they capture the miraculous experience of being alive.

Understanding the depth of the suffering Jews have endured in their history leads us to open ourselves to both mourning and celebrating, crying and laughing—but especially crying.

It is strange that we cry in moments of pain but also in moments of intense joy. What do pain and joy have in common that they can both move us to tears? Both pain and joy can bring us face-to-face with the bedrock of life, and this encounter is overwhelming. Suddenly it hits us:

This moment is real and life is overwhelmingly mysterious, miraculous, and incomprehensible. Our intellectual and emotional faculties, with which we generally grasp reality, are simply too small to capture the truth we face, and we break down in tears. This is hinted at in the metaphoric language of the Kabbalah that describes how, at the beginning of creation, the finite vessels of human perception broke down because they could not contain the endless light of God's truth.

I used to imagine that, someday, when I would stand under the wedding canopy, the *chupa*, of my children, I would be crying my eyes out. And sure enough, that's what has happened. When you really open yourself up to the deepest, most powerful experiences that life offers, you cannot help crying.

Jeremiah, while lamenting the destruction of the Temple, tells us, "Pour out your heart like water." It is interesting that tears are salty. Saltwater does not quench your thirst; rather, it makes you thirstier. However, Jeremiah is teaching us that when tears pour out of our hearts, then such tears actually satiate us like fresh water.

Crying from the heart satisfies a very deep need—it quenches. The psychologist Carl Jung said that neurosis is a substitute for legitimate suffering. In other words, denial of our pain is counterproductive and even destructive. If we are not ready to accept our legitimate suffering, then we will express it in unhealthy and dysfunctional ways. However, acknowledging our sadness and expressing it heals our hurt, helps turn our pain into a source of motivation, and empowers us to feel joy with even greater sensitivity.

To be fully alive means to open ourselves up to the spectrum of life's experiences and to embrace the dance of pain and pleasure, joy and sadness, laughter and tears.

The secret is not to be happy but to be whole. Wholeness, however, is actually the true path to real happiness, because when you are whole, you experience an inner happiness even in times of sadness. You take pleasure in your ability to feel pain. You embrace and celebrate the totality of your humanness. But to be whole, you must be willing to immerse yourself in the complete drama of being alive and human.

Therefore, even as I struggle to share Jewish pain with my children, I feel a strange joy in it. It gives me a deep sense of peace to share with my children this battle, this restlessness that Jews feel, because this is truly the path to wholeness and experiencing the fullness of life.

THE CRYING OF TISHA B'AV

On Tisha B'Av, a day fraught with tragedy in Jewish history, we have many reasons to cry. On the surface we cry over the destruction of the Temple, which was destroyed twice on this day.

For most people, however, it is difficult to really feel pain over the destruction of the Temple, because when we hear the word *Temple*, we think of some synagogue down the street—a far cry from what the Holy Temple of Jerusalem was like. Physically, it was considered one of the wonders of the ancient world, but its true value was spiritual. Because the Temple was a source of tremendous spiritual light that radiated out to the world, its window shafts were inverted to allow the light from within to shine out. The Temple did not need the natural light of the outside world; the world needed the supernatural light of the Temple.

Speaking about natural light, King Solomon declared in the book of Ecclesiastes, "Futility of futilities, of what worth is the work of man under the sun." In other words, when you look at daily life in the light of nature, it often looks futile, mundane, sometimes even silly or absurd. But there is a higher light—a transcendental spiritual light. And in that light nothing we do could ever be futile, because it reveals the godliness within each of us and within everything we do. When the Temple was destroyed, this spiritual light and the precious clarity of godliness it revealed were destroyed along with it.

On Tisha B'Av we are not mourning over a building. We did not simply lose a great work of architecture. The Temple reminded us that we are the living sanctuary for the presence of God on earth—God as manifest within us and within the world. God Himself made this clear to Moses, when He directed the Israelites to build for him a portable Tabernacle, which eventually became a permanent Temple: "Build for Me a sanctuary and I will dwell among them." When the nation of Israel lost touch with this fundamental reason for the Temple's existence, the Temple was destroyed.

The Jewish oral tradition teaches that when the invaders destroyed the Temple, God said that they only destroyed a building that was already in ruins. The Temple was really the externalization of our inner awareness—our spiritual orientation toward each other and toward God. When we spiritually denied the presence of God within ourselves and within each other, the external manifestation of this truth—the Temple—had no meaning. Therefore, the Temple could not remain standing once the meaning of what it stood for was lost.

The Jewish oral tradition also teaches that when the Temple was destroyed, the Shekhinah (the Divine Presence on earth) "departed to heaven," and now an "iron wall separates the children of Israel from God." And because of this, there is no laughter before God, the sky is no longer seen in its purity, the taste, fragrance, and nourishing quality of fruit has been lost, the enjoyment of sex has been taken away, and God only dwells within the "four cubits of Jewish Law."

How can we understand this?

The Kabbalah teaches that God is paradoxically both beyond and yet within us and the physical world. He is simultaneously transcendent and immanent. Therefore, although heaven and earth—the spiritual and the physical—are opposites, they are not in opposition. They are one. In addition, the Kabbalah explains that our true inner self, the soul, is godly, and therefore we are only attracted to, and derive ultimate pleasure from, the godliness within the physical world and within each other. Therefore, the more we are in touch with ourselves as souls, the more we are attuned to the godliness within the physical, the more sensual we become, and the more pleasure we experience.

The presence of the Temple and the message it conveyed expressed this mystical truth about God and ourselves. However, when the nation of Israel—the very caretakers of the Temple—negated this truth, the Temple lost its true meaning and then, inevitably, it was destroyed.

Therefore, we are taught that when the Temple was destroyed, the Shekhinah "departed to heaven." In other words, the destruction of the Temple means that we perceive God as transcendent and removed from us and the physical world. We now feel an "iron wall" separating us from godliness. And because we have disconnected ourselves and the physical world from God, everything seems so trivial; we have lost the ability to truly laugh and enjoy life. The sky has lost its heavenly luster and can no longer be seen in its purity. We have numbed our taste buds and lost our true sensuality, which derived only from the soul's awareness of the presence of God within the physical. Therefore, the taste, fragrance, and nourishing quality of fruit is lost. Even sexual pleasure is gone. Now, unfortunately, we can only find God within the confines of matters addressed by Torah law when, in truth, His splendorous presence also fills the entire world.

In other words, with the destruction of the Temple our sensitivity to the Divine Presence within this world and within each other was almost totally lost, and with it, the ultimate vitality and true pleasures of life and love.

Therefore, on Tisha B'Av, we do not cry over real

estate but over our real and sad state as a people. The physical Temple can exist only when we are the living sanctuary for the presence of God and acknowledge that presence within each other and within the world.

Practically, if I really felt that you were a sanctuary—that within you dwells a spirit of godliness—then I would treat you the way I would treat God. Not only would I say hello to you, I would say it with such joy, such excitement and love, that you would be reminded of the godly soul that you are.

When we forget the godliness in ourselves, in others, and in the world—when we do not make ourselves and our daily lives into a sanctuary to receive God's presence—then buildings do not make any difference. How many synagogues can we enter today and feel the presence of God? In how many synagogues can we truly feel we are learning Torah, really praying, sincerely welcoming and inviting each other and God into our lives?

The Talmud says that every generation that does not witness the rebuilding of the Temple is considered as if it had destroyed the Temple. Simply, if we do not merit having the Temple, then it is an indication that we continue to shut out the presence of God from ourselves and from the world. We must transform ourselves into a living sanctuary for God before the Temple in Jerusalem can be rebuilt.

THE TRAGEDY OF OUR TIMES

Perhaps the greatest tragedy and loss that we should mourn during Tisha B'Av is that today most of us are not feeling any tragedy or loss. Most of us are not mourning on Tisha B'Av, and we hardly know on what day of the year the ninth of Av occurs. We need to cry over the fact that we are not crying.

This lack of awareness is referred to in Hebrew as *hester hester panim*, "the hiddenness of the hidden face of God." There are two levels of God's hiddenness: the obvious and the double-blind. If you are playing hide-and-seek and someone is hiding from you, you obviously know that you need to be looking for that someone. But another level of hiding is when you don't even know to look. This is the lowest level of God-consciousness, because we are not even aware that God and godliness are missing from our lives. And this is a tragedy today— many of us are not even looking for God.

The Hasidic master Rabbi Nachman of Breslav taught, "There is nothing more whole than a broken heart." How could your heart not be broken when you face the sad state of the world today? A person whose heart breaks over the lack of awareness of godliness in the world is truly a wholehearted person.

I was once invited to San Francisco to speak to a group of people who were recovering from a variety of addictions. Before I spoke, everyone in the room shared their particular problem. I was humbled before so much holiness. What was so holy about these people? Their broken hearts.

These people were confronting their brokenness and seeking productive ways to deal with it. They knew that something was missing in their lives, and they were pained by the emptiness. They knew that only when they embraced the legitimacy of their suffering and acknowledged that only God, rather than their addictions, could fill the hole in their lives would they be empowered to make changes and become healthy.

Most of us today are not sad on Tisha B'Av; most of us don't mourn the destruction of the Temple, because we don't confront the emptiness and pain in our lives. Our lack of desire for the Temple is the inner tragedy of Tisha B'Av. The Temple fills a need, and yet most of us do not know what that need is. We are oblivious to the need for God's presence in our lives. Before the Temple can be rebuilt, we must know why we need the Temple and why we should desperately want it.

THE TEARS OF GOD

There is a searing story related in the Midrash that describes God in a state of agony. "Woe, what have I done?" God wails. "I have destroyed the Temple; I have cast out my children! What have I done?"

An angel comes to God and says, "Do not cry, God. Let me cry your tears and reveal them to the world."

"No, I will go into My inner chamber and I will cry there," God tells the angel. And He does just that. He enters His inner chamber, locks the door, and cries because He misses and wants the Temple.

But if God really missed the Temple, you may be wondering, what would stop Him from rebuilding it? If God really wanted this, why would He not bring the redemption now? This question is similar to the often-asked question: If God really cared about the Jewish people, where was He during the Holocaust?

According to this Midrash, God was in His inner chamber crying, concealing His tears.

One Tisha B'Av several years ago, I shared this story with a group of students. One of the participants was a fellow named Tom. The son of two Holocaust survivors, Tom was deeply immersed in Holocaust studies, and he was passionately angry with God. I was amazed that he even participated in the program, but for some reason something drew him to it.

Afterward, he approached me and said, "You know, Rabbi, I've been waiting so long for a rabbi to tell me that God is crying. Now I can cry with God, rather than be angry at Him."

Tom understood that the ways of God are beyond our human comprehension, and the tragic events in Jewish history often remain a painful mystery. But nonetheless he was disturbed by the image of God sitting in His "ivory tower," watching us suffer. How could a loving, compassionate father stoically observe the suffering of his children? But now it dawned on him that God experienced our pain also.

If Jews knew just how much God is still crying, there would be many more like Tom, joining God in His tears. Most people imagine a powerful God emotionlessly looking at us from heaven above. But Rabbi Kalymous Kalman Shapira, who was the rabbi of the Warsaw ghetto and eventually perished in a concentration camp, described God as having "endless pain." Our pain is limited because we are limited beings. But in His infinitude, God's pain is endless.

UNDERSTANDING GOD'S PAIN

It is very difficult for us to understand why God is in pain and what He is doing crying in His inner chamber. Further, why would the angel—as described in the Midrash—want to cry God's tears and reveal them to the world?

According to Rabbi Shapira, the angel knew that if God's tears were to be revealed in this world, then the whole world would be destroyed. If we were to hear God crying, if we knew how pained God was over the state of this world, we would be filled with torturous shame, so much so that we could not go on living. Our inability to handle God's pain is the reason God is compassionately hiding it from us.

Now we can begin to fathom that when we experience a lack of intervention from God, it is not a sign of insensitive abandonment—it is actually a sign of compassionate divine repression. Sometimes humanity stoops to such a low level of ethical behavior that, should God respond with justice, the world would necessarily be destroyed. Therefore, God hides—so to speak—in His chamber, because if God were to allow His pain to become manifest in this world, we could not take it. In other words, because we are in such denial of God's pain over the cruel acts of humanity, experiencing it would so devastate us that we would die on the spot. We are not ready or willing to acknowledge and feel God's pain.

Now, you may wonder, if having a Temple would stop God from crying, then it would seem logical for God simply to rebuild the Temple.

But He can't.

God cannot rebuild the Temple in Jerusalem unless we want it and the spiritual meaning it represents. Practically speaking, there is no point in the Temple unless we want to embody the presence of God in our lives and acknowledge the godliness within each other. There is no point in bringing the Jewish people back to the Promised Land of Israel unless we acknowledge it as a Holy Land, where God's presence can be felt among us.

This last point reminds me of the first time I met Kirk Douglas. When he arrived in Israel, government executives took him on an official tour to show the famous Jewish actor the beauty of Jerusalem. Their first stop was the mall.

"Quite frankly, Rabbi, it was a very unimpressive mall," he later told me.

Then they took him to the so-called Biblical Zoo to see a few Bible verses written in animal cages. "Rabbi," he said to me, "I hate zoos. I don't like animals being in cages."

As the grand finale, they took him to the new soccer stadium.

What they did not do was plan anything of a spiritual nature for the man, never dreaming that he would want such a thing. For some crazy reason, I sent him a note inviting him for Shabbat dinner, and for some crazy reason he accepted. I could not figure out why a great actor would come to my home, since surely he must have had some specially organized VIP Shabbat dinner planned. But no, they gave him that evening off.

As it turned out, that Shabbat dinner at my home provided the genuine feeling he was looking for and was the spiritual highlight of his trip. He later wrote about his experience in his book *Climbing the Mountain*:

> We ate a delicious meal and sang songs with the rabbi beating time on the table. Through the window, I could see other houses lit by the warm light of candles and could hear the same songs echoing in the night. They were happy songs. I felt good. That night I felt that I had come home.

For Kirk Douglas, "coming home" was not going to the Jerusalem Mall—coming home was connecting with God through the special experience of a Shabbat in Jerusalem. This is what was missing on the VIP tour.

If we really understood what we were missing, we would be bawling our eyes out over the fact that we are not home, that we are in exile, and that the Temple has not been rebuilt. We would be yearning for it and for God's presence among us.

What we are missing, however, is not the building. It is the awareness that a greater presence is absent from our lives. A consciousness of God—a desire for God in our everyday life—is gone.

God cannot rebuild the Temple until we want God in our lives and need a Temple to express that holy desire. The Temple remains in ruins because we do not yet want God in our lives enough to warrant a Temple. And this is why God is crying.

DEVELOPING GOD-CONSCIOUSNESS

Awareness of God's presence is not some metaphysical or philosophical endeavor, nor is it reserved for just meditating or chanting. Achieving true God-consciousness starts with recognizing the godliness within others, and greeting and treating them accordingly.

Some of my students come from Orthodox Jewish homes, yet they do not believe in God. Their parents cannot figure out what went wrong, considering that they sent their kids to yeshivas and heard them reciting the Shema and other prayers daily. On the other hand, some of my students are intense believers, yet they come from atheistic homes. Their parents cannot figure out what went wrong—how their children became so religious.

Sometimes the answer is simple. There are people who say they believe in God yet treat people like dirt. If they really believed in God, they would not treat people like dirt. There are also people who say they do not believe in God, and yet they treat every human being with respect and sensitivity, as though each person was created in the image of God. These people act like believers. Behaving as though there is a God is what Judaism means by God-consciousness. And the way we behave is the way we really communicate our beliefs to our children.

To want a Temple means to want to live in a world with God-consciousness. And we must desire to behave in concert with that awareness. We have to want to treat people with the sensitivity that would be symptomatic of such awareness.

The absence of this understanding is what keeps God crying and stops Him from rebuilding the Temple. Not enough people in the world want the Temple. They are not ready to live in a world filled with the presence of God and act accordingly.

THE PAIN OF GODLESSNESS

Releasing God from His pain requires us not only to change our behavior. We must also stop being preoccupied with our own pain and the reasons for it. According to Judaism, there is only one reason for all our pain: we are in pain because we do not have God in our lives. The pain is there only to inspire us to turn to God and invite Him into our lives. And the more we invite God into everything we are and do, the less pain and the more joy we feel.

The Talmud tells a story about Rabbi Yossi, who, while walking in Jerusalem, heard God crying. "Woe unto Me!" God sobbed. "I have destroyed my house . . . I have burned the Temple . . . I have exiled my children!" The

Talmud tells this story to point out something special about Rabbi Yossi that enabled him to hear God's cries—he was able to get past his own pain.

When we get beyond our own personal, egotistical problems, we can hear the cry of God.

Sometimes I hear a cry within myself that I cannot figure out. Everything is fine, I may be having a nice discussion with someone, and I hear an inner crying. When this happens, I do not panic. I know that these moments are opportunities to delve deeper inside myself to find God.

Only by exploring our innermost depths can we hear God crying. Popular belief is that the opposite is true—that we have to search far beyond ourselves to see and hear God. When the first Russian cosmonaut reached outer space, the first thing he said was, "I don't see God." Where did he think God was?

We do not meet God in outer space. We meet God in inner space. And the deeper we are willing to go, the closer we come to the root of our soul—the aspect of God within each of us. The closer we get to the root of our soul, the louder we will hear the crying.

One of the reasons people would rather live in a superficial world and not delve deeper is because they are afraid of confronting the pain. These people are forgetting that we do not resolve pain by denying it. We can only resolve pain by expressing it through our tears.

We are not crying with God, because we have not explored our inner selves. We have not returned to the essence, to the root, of who we are. Deep inside our souls, all human beings are crying over the fact that we are not really living like godly beings, we are not treating each other according to our godliness. Essentially, we are not letting God into our lives.

On Tisha B'Av we mourn on a few levels. On a historical level, we mourn over the past—what was and what no longer is. On a deeper level, we mourn over what could have been. But on a much more profound level, we mourn over the fact that we are not mourning enough. We cry over the fact that we are not crying enough. To fix this we need to delve deep inside and listen carefully to hear God crying.

FINDING GOD THROUGH TEARS

Before we can hear God crying, we have to improve our listening.

One of the reasons we do not hear each other—much less God—is that we are constantly thinking about what we want to say rather than listening to what someone else is saying to us. We are talking to ourselves in our heads the whole time someone else is talking to us.

To put it simply, we need to stop talking so much. Judaism teaches that we must take time for silence. We can hear God's voice from the depths of our soul only when we are quiet—when we stop talking and start listening. If we were to listen deep inside ourselves, rather than running away from it, we would hear the crying. And we would cry too—not our own tears, but God's tears.

God's tears are the tears that come from deep down,

from the godliness within you. These tears are not salty. You will know that they are God's tears when they are actually quenching your thirst, as God's presence enters your life. And with this new God-awareness you will act, speak, and think in more caring and loving ways.

Tisha B'Av reminds you that you have to get more real with yourself. What in your life is worth crying over? What is worth being pained about? What is really missing, and what do you really want?

When each one of us answers these questions, we will understand the true meaning of Tisha B'Av, and we will discover our ultimate dreams and our deepest desires. And then we will celebrate our loss and sadness because recognizing what is missing and knowing what truly makes us sad is the path to finding the greatest happiness—finding what we truly want.

On Tisha B'Av we discover that what is really missing and all that we truly want is love—love for God and each other.

—FOUR—

Rosh Hashanah

Celebrating Accountability

There is a Hasidic teaching that the soul is like a rare and valuable coin that can become tarnished and lose its luster without proper care. However, if we shine and polish it, it becomes brilliant again. And when our soul— our true self—shines, we are happy.

The month of Tishrei, the period of the Jewish calendar that includes Rosh Hashanah, Yom Kippur, Sukkot, and Simchat Torah, is a time when we polish our tarnished souls to reveal our true radiance and experience the joy of being who we really are. Because the soul is actually an aspect of God, the more we are in touch with our soul the more we experience our connection with

God. True happiness comes with the discovery of our innate godliness and oneness with God.

According to Kabbalah, life is an evolving process of awareness whereby we gradually discover who we really are and how we have always been one with God and with each other. The realization of this oneness is the experience of love, and this is the greatest joy we can ever feel.

The great sixteenth-century master of the Kabbalah, Rabbi Isaac Luria—better known as the Ari—explains that the story of Adam and Eve is a paradigm for understanding this process of awareness, especially in reference to what is spiritually happening during the High Holidays.

The Torah teaches that Adam was not just a man; he was androgynous, both male and female, connected back-to-back. Neither part knew the other existed. After creating this being, God said that it is not good for Adam to be alone. To help him find his match—*eizer kanegdo*, literally, "a helper opposite to him"—God charged Adam with naming all the animals. Essentially, God was setting up Adam, so to speak, on blind dates in the lobby of the Garden of Eden Hotel. Adam was waiting there anxiously, thinking, "Maybe this is the one for me." In walks a giraffe. "No," thinks Adam. "This is a giraffe. Maybe God is warming up." Then in walks a gorilla, and so on, until poor Adam has named all the animals. Feeling no connection on these blind dates, he became increasingly lonely and despondent.

The Torah then relates that God put Adam to sleep. Some Torah commentators say that Adam actually went to sleep because he was depressed (a feeling I still remember well from my own dating days). While Adam was sleeping, God separated the two beings, though some commentators say that God removed a rib from his side in order to separate the two. In either case, Adam woke up to find his other half, Eve, whom he realized was of his essence. At this point, Adam and Eve stood face-to-face, chose to unite, and experienced the ecstasy of love.

Originally, they were back-to-back—one being, but not conscious of that truth. And they certainly did not experience love, because to experience love they had to—through challenge and choice—become conscious of their oneness.

The Ari explains the story of Adam and Eve as the quintessential love story, which parallels the love story between us and God. Just as in the case of Adam and Eve, we experience the feelings of loneliness and alienation that actually create the yearning and the anticipation for the final conscious reuniting with God.

THE CHOICE TO CONNECT TO GOD

Similar to Adam and Eve—who began as one entity joined back-to-back yet knew nothing of each other's existence—we too are intrinsically connected to God whether we know it or not. But without knowing it, we cannot experience the blissful joy of oneness. Until we experience alienation from God, yearn for oneness, and consciously choose to reconnect to God, until we move from being back-to-back to being face-to-face with God, we will not know the ecstasy of ultimate love.

We experience intrinsic connection with people almost daily. For example, at those times when we show kindness to another person, the amount of connection we feel with that person may far surpass our good deed. Similarly, when we meet our soul mate, we may feel as if we have known him or her for many years. The reason for these feelings of connectedness is that we are not only one with God, but we are all one with each other—we just do not know we are one. Our challenge is to make the right choices and behave in ways that will reveal the oneness that we already existentially share.

This means that we do not have to do anything to earn our connection to God. And we do not have to earn God's love. We are one with Him this very moment, and that connection can never be broken no matter what we do. Our only problem is that we do not live a lifestyle that enables us to feel that truth. We have to behave in ways that acknowledge our oneness with God and experience God's love. All the commandments of the Torah empower us to know this truth and experience the love we share with God.

When we are not conscious of our oneness with God and one another, we feel at a loss. We feel alienated, sad, and lonely. In truth, we would never feel lonely if we had never been connected in the first place. You cannot miss something that you never had. We may feel sad, lonely, removed, distanced, and alienated from people and God—even though we are all actually one—because our choices and behavior contradict that truth. When we behave in ways that do not affirm this oneness—like when we transgress a Torah commandment or when we act as if we are our own gods, determining for ourselves what is good and what is evil—we are actually violating the truth of our oneness and begin to feel disconnected from God and others. When we do a mitzvah, when we choose to follow God's commandments, we reveal our oneness with God and others. We then begin to feel the mutual love between us, the greatest joy possible.

CONNECTING TO THE HOLIDAYS

The High Holidays that begin the Jewish year enable us to discover this truth and experience love and joy to the utmost. According to the Kabbalah, the period beginning with Rosh Hashanah, extending into Yom Kippur, followed by the festival of Sukkot and ending with Simchat Torah, is an especially opportune time for realizing our ultimate and eternal connection to God and to each other. This period is the foundation upon which our entire year is built.

Each Rosh Hashanah, the Kabbalah explains, we return to a state of back-to-back with God—we are one with Him, but we do not know it. We yearn to return to God during the ten days of awe from Rosh Hashanah to Yom Kippur, the day on which we are finally granted forgiveness. It is that forgiveness that reestablishes and reveals our face-to-face connection, and the joy of that forgiveness empowers us to achieve the ultimate realization of our oneness with God on Simchat Torah. Every year we repeat the cycle—back-to-back and face-to-face with God—but not every year do we experience the same joy. As time passes and the awareness of our oneness with God becomes clearer and stronger, we experience an even deeper connection and an even greater love and joy.

Think about it this way: When you really love some-one, over time you realize how much more there is to love of that person. Every year, you look back at the last year and say, "We thought we were in love? We thought we were expressing our connection? Nothing compares to the love and connection we now experience." When you work on a relationship, you can reveal even deeper levels of connectedness. One of the worst things that could happen in a relationship is that a husband and wife wake up one day, look at each other, and say, "You know what? We did it. I love you and you love me." Love is not a destiny—it is an endless journey. You never arrive. There is always more to love. There are always deeper dimensions of oneness and connectedness that are wait-ing to be revealed through kind words, kind deeds, shar-ing, and communicating.

On each Rosh Hashanah a whole new level of love is available—beyond what was accomplished last year. The love we experienced last year, relative to the potential of the love available this year, is as if we are once again back-to-back with God—connected but not aware of the connection and not feeling the joy and excitement of that love. We are as if in a state of sleep, unconscious of who we are and how connected we are to God, just like

Adam before he met and faced his soul mate. We blow the shofar on Rosh Hashanah to awaken us from our unconsciousness so that we can begin to face God and return to love. But how can we face God when we also wake up to the truth that we have violated our connection to Him? We feel so small—dwarfed by our wrongdoings of the past year.

THE JUDGMENT

I guess this must be why there is a part of me that really dislikes Rosh Hashanah. I find being judged to be a very uncomfortable experience—not pleasurable at all. Rosh Hashanah is *Yom HaDin*, the Day of Judgment, and I simply dread being judged. Who enjoys feeling threatened? Who enjoys fearing punishment? Rosh Hashanah is also *Yom HaZicharon*, the Day of Memory. On this day God remembers everything—every little itsy-bitsy teeny-weeny little thing that I did last year—and then decides my fate for the upcoming year.

There is, however, another part of me that feels very good about Rosh Hashanah. I know that it's an opportunity to take inventory of my actions, reflect, and make changes to improve myself and my relationships. Viewed from that perspective, judgment is actually empowering. It tells me that God cares about my choices and that I make a difference in this world.

The book of Psalms summarizes my ambivalence: "Serve God with reverence, rejoice in trembling." The Talmudic sages associate this verse with Rosh Hashanah.

But doesn't this seem a contradiction? It makes sense that either I am happy and rejoicing, or I am frightened and trembling, but how can I be doing and feeling both at the same time?

Yet on Rosh Hashanah somehow I am rejoicing about my trembling.

To really understand this paradox, let's explore what Rosh Hashanah really means. What is this Day of Judgment, this Day of Memory, when the shofar, the ram's horn, is blown like a trumpet?

Rosh Hashanah reveals the classic monotheistic image of God. God is the one and only King; He decrees the rules for His Kingdom and He enforces them. If we do not abide by His rules, then we must bear the consequences. On Rosh Hashanah the King holds court and judges us. We blow the shofar to announce the coming of the King and the commencement of the trial.

All year long, our ego may feel confident and strong. It convinces us that we can do what we want, when we want, and where we want. We think that we are self-defined, independent beings who are not accountable to a Higher Power. We believe that we can judge for ourselves what is right and wrong. But when Rosh Hashanah comes, we are reminded that there's a King to whom we are accountable—a King who determines what is right and wrong and who judges us. When the King comes, our egos are threatened, and we tremble. The ego realizes that it is living a lie and it must fess up: "I am not independent, and there is a Higher Power whom I must obey and who judges me. I am not the king, and I am not the judge."

However, even though my ego is shaken, my soul rejoices. The judgment overwhelms my ego but empowers my true inner self—my soul. The coming of the King, while challenging my ego, ironically confirms my sense of self. Knowing that the King judges me assures me that my choices and actions make a difference to God—that my existence, and the way I choose to live my life, really matter to Him.

THE KINDNESS OF JUDGMENT

The Psalmist teaches, "God, unto You is kindness, for You pay a person according to his deeds." This doesn't seem to make sense. God is kind because He pays a person according to his deeds? Paying a person according to his deeds is not kindness, it is justice. Kindness should be defined as paying whether the person deserves it or not.

The biblical story of Abraham's servant, Eliezar, helps us understand what kindness is. Eliezar was sent by Abraham to find a wife for Abraham's son, Isaac. A young woman, Rebecca, caught Eliezar's eye, but upon first glance it was not clear to him whether this woman was the appropriate wife for his master's son. He decided she would be the right one if she demonstrated the virtue of kindness. Therefore, he asked her for some water, and she responded by bringing water not only for him but for his ten camels as well. She was certainly not obligated to fetch water for Eliezar, let alone his camels. But when she did so, it became clear that she was very kind.

Justice is very different from kindness. Justice is giving you what you deserve. For example, if I damage your car, it is not an act of kindness on my part if I pay for the repairs—it is an act of justice. You deserve to be paid, and I owe you.

But when I do something for you even though, from the standpoint of judgment, you do not deserve it—and there are even good reasons for me not to do this for you—that's something else altogether: that's compassion. For instance, let's say you borrow my car and damage it, and then ask to use it again. Even though I may have a good reason not to lend it to you, I may choose to be compassionate, forgive you, and say OK. Compassion is kindness overriding justice.

To sum it up: Judgment means I do something for you because you deserve it and I am beholden to you. Kindness means I help you even though I do not owe it to you—I do it because I want to. Compassion means I help you even though you don't deserve my help, in fact you actually deserve to be punished; nonetheless I do not seek justice but instead act favorably toward you.

In light of this, how can we now understand the verse from Psalms: "God, unto You is kindness, for You pay a person according to his deeds"? This verse teaches us that the true source of God's justice is kindness. God judges us *because* He is kind.

I learned that justice is kindness from my mother. When I was five years old, I got very upset with her, and, in a fit of anger, I took out all of her stockings and tied them together into little knots. "I showed her," I thought, feeling very proud of myself. However, as soon as I heard my mother coming, I quickly hid my masterpiece in the china cabinet. Of course, I got caught. My mother opened up the china cabinet and, sure enough, found all her stockings tied into little knots.

She said, "David, I found something very bizarre. My stockings somehow got into the china cabinet."

"Oh, yeah? How did they get there?" I responded in mock astonishment.

"Not only are they in the china cabinet," she said, "but they are full of knots."

"Wow! Who did that?"

Needless to say, my mother knew who did it, and I was punished accordingly.

But imagine that my mother had found her stockings all in knots and said, "Oh, how nice. Look at that. What creativity! Did you do that?"

And imagine that when I, shaking with fear, admitted it, she said, "Don't worry, it's OK. I can buy more stockings. It doesn't matter."

If that had happened, how would I have felt? Even at age five, I would have realized on some level that my actions were insignificant and meaningless to my mother. If she had responded in that way, I would have felt much worse than I did being punished.

We can live with punishment, but we cannot live without meaning; we cannot live knowing that our choices and actions are inconsequential. Therefore, an act of judgment that brings home the point that we matter can be, in fact, an act of kindness.

Sometimes children actually want to be judged. There are times when my children do something wrong and then look at me as if daring me to punish them. It's written all over their faces. Sometimes they will misbehave and continue to misbehave even after I've warned them that I will punish them if they don't stop. Children want to see that their actions really make a difference. They want to feel the power of their choices and experience how great the consequences of their behavior can be. This is one of the ways that children test their parents to see if they really love and care about them. Judgment actually builds a child's self-esteem. Some parents fear that if they judge or punish their child, then he will think that his mother and father do not love him. However, just the opposite is true. Judaism teaches that parents who do not discipline their children hate their children. Punishment gives children an opportunity to discover their personal boundaries. It confirms to them that they are powerful, that there are consequences to their actions and their choices matter.

One of my teachers once made a very strong statement that took me a while to appreciate. He said, "People are free in a box." We all need a box. Outside of a box, without some kind of framework or personal limits and boundaries, we lack definition and we get lost in space. If anything goes, nothing goes, because then nothing we do makes a difference.

I saw a cute comic strip once. It showed a guy in a box.

His whole life he tried to get out of his box and be free. Eventually, he figured out how to construct a contraption that helped him leap over the walls. But the funny thing was that he was actually still in a box because cartoons have a border around them. Such is the nature of freedom—freedom is really about getting out of one box into another box. There is never a time when we are living without boundaries or some frame of reference. If our choices did not have consequences, then there would be no possibility for freedom, and we would have no sense of personal power or significance.

For children, part of growing up and discovering themselves is discovering boundaries. They naturally want to know what they can and can't do. They need to test their limits, learn the consequences, and discover the reward or punishment for their actions. When they err, when they are out of bounds, they are punished accordingly, so that they can get back in line.

How this works is illustrated by the Hebrew word for judgment, *mishpat*, which also means "sentence." It is interesting to note that, even in English, we use terminology like "being sentenced" to describe judgment and punishment. What is the connection between justice and a sentence? When we misbehave we are acting out of line. Our actions are out of context with the real theme of life. Therefore, the judge has to get us back in line by giving us some kind of corrective sentence. Punishment is not for its own sake—punishment gets us back on track.

I have met people who clearly have never been disciplined. This is apparent because they demonstrate how little self-worth they have. They do not believe that their choices and actions really make a difference, and therefore they are indecisive and unmotivated. They lack clarity about where the borders of behavior lie, and they lack the confidence necessary to make a move. Of course, some people suffer low self-esteem precisely because they were punished too much. Such individuals have lost hope in their ability to do anything right. Parents need to relate to their children in a balanced way. Too little judgment or too much judgment will damage a child's feeling of self-worth and confidence. This is one of the great challenges of parenthood. In order to be an effective parent you need to know your own boundaries as well as the boundaries of your relationship with your children. As a parent, you have to know when it's time to rebuke and when it's time to forgive and forget. Often kids complain that their parents criticize them too much. They may even wonder, "Do my parents love me?" Of course it is precisely because the parents care so much about their children that they are so critical of them: they want to see them grow up and become the best they can be.

If you are walking down the street and you see a stranger's son eating ice cream, and it is all over his face and all over his shirt, you are not going to walk up to him and say, "Come on kid, get a napkin!" It's not your child, and you don't really care so much about other kids' grooming. But if it's your own child, you really care.

True judgment is actually an act of loving-kindness. When I judge my child, I am giving him a sense of self-worth; I am instilling within him the confidence that he is a powerful person, that his choices are significant and consequential. I am assuring him that his actions make a difference, that he matters, and that I love him. We have a kind of paradoxical experience on Rosh Hashanah: there is tremendous pain, yet there is also tremendous pleasure. On Rosh Hashanah, when I acknowledge that God is the one and only King and Judge, my ego feels overwhelmed. My illusion of being self-contained, without any accountability to a Higher Power, is shattered. This egotistical illusion is what the Kabbalah calls a *klipah*, a hard shell. When the shell is broken, I realize that I cannot do whatever I want, whenever or wherever I want. I am not independent and self-defined. There is someone to whom I am accountable. That is very frightening to my ego, but very reassuring to my inner self. My self wants to feel accountable, because if I am not accountable then I don't count. Therefore, on Rosh Hashanah, while my pained ego shatters into little pieces, my true inner self—the soul—is strengthened and rejoices.

On Rosh Hashanah I know that God's judgment is actually an expression of His great love and care for me.

THE MEANING OF THE SHOFAR

When we blow the shofar, we start off with a long blast announcing the coming of the King and the establishment of His ruling power. Then the shofar is sounded again—a few shorter, fragmented blasts, which reflect the breakdown of the ego. The King's presence over-whelms the ego, and it breaks down. Then, strangely enough, out of the breakdown comes a new strength—another longer blast—that hints at the empowerment of the self. This is one interpretation of the variations in the sounds of the shofar.

The first sound is called in Hebrew *tekiah*, which means "to sound a horn," but it also means "to drive a stake firmly into the ground." In other words, this sound signals to us that we must firmly establish in our hearts the truth that God is the one and only King and true Judge. The next sound is a broken, staccato sound re-ferred to in general as *Truah*. The Talmud struggles to define the exact nature of this sound: it is either a sighing sound similar to three groans of sadness (in Hebrew, *shev-arim*, which literally means *breakings*), or a wailing sound similar to nine sobs of distress (in Hebrew, *truah*), or a combination of both together. This hints at the break-down of the *klipah*, the hard shell created by our ego, which claims that we are self-contained and independent of God. However, after the ego is shattered, we once again hear the *tekiah*, now expressing the empowerment of the self. We are strong and confident, standing in the loving presence of God. God's judgment actually affirms our power to make a difference, the truth that we matter and that He loves us.

The sounding of the shofar accompanies three themes that we express in the prayers on Rosh Hashanah: *malchiot* ("kingship"), *zichronot* ("memories"), and *shofrot* ("sounds of the shofar").

Malchiot means that God is the King. He is our King, He rules over us all because He created the world, and He created us. This world is His kingdom, and we are His subjects.

Even though God is our King and next to Him we may feel comparatively minute, *zichronot* remind us that we are great in the eyes of God. He remembers us and watches over us. God takes note of everything we do, because each and every one of us is significant and note-worthy in His eyes. He is our King and we are His subjects; He cares about us, and therefore we are the subject of His rule and love. He only wants whatever is in our best interest, unlike a tyrant or dictator who treats his people like objects and uses them for his own interest and pleasure. *Zichronot* affirm that God remembers us and never forgets us. If there are times in our lives when we feel forgotten, this is only from our perspective—God always remembers us, watches over us, and cares.

The third theme expressed in the Rosh Hashanah prayers is *shofrot*; it refers to the sounds of the shofar heard at the time of the giving of the Torah at Mount Sinai. *Shofrot* affirm our belief that God not only loves us and cares about us, but He gave us a way to love Him and care about the manifestation of His presence on earth—through the commandments of the Torah. Through the mitzvot we are able to love and bond with Him. This is the meaning of the teachings of the Torah and the ultimate purpose of the commandments it contains.

When the Israelites heard the blast of the shofar at Mount Sinai, they were simply blown away (forgive the pun). The Midrash teaches that the immensity and intensity of the revelation was so great that everyone simply died on the spot. Therefore, God sent angels to push the souls of the Israelites back into their bodies and revived them. Although they were totally devastated by the revelation of God, He gave them the strength to stand in His presence.

These same dynamics are at work on Rosh Hashanah. On the one hand, we feel frightened and threatened; on the other hand, there is something very affirming in knowing that the King cares, that our choices matter to Him, and that His judgment will guide us toward choosing the greatest good—a life of Torah and mitzvot—so that we can enjoy life's greatest pleasure: bonding with God.

THE BIRTHDAY OF HUMANITY

Rosh Hashanah, the Day of Judgment, is actually the day that humanity was created. It is the birthday of the first human beings, Adam and Eve. Why do we celebrate our collective birthday at a time when we are being judged in the court of God? Not quite the fun birthday party that we might have hoped for.

Of course, whether it's a fun day or a down day depends on how we choose to perceive the meaning of a birthday. Little children get so excited about their birthdays; they talk about them and plan for them months in advance. To them, a birthday says, "I am special. I was born today, and everybody celebrates the great event of my coming into the world." But the truth is, as we get older, we begin to wonder if anybody really wants to celebrate our birthday. Does anybody really care? We also tend to ask ourselves painful questions: Does my existence matter at all? What have I done with my life? What am I living for? So, in essence, a birthday is actually a day of judgment. We judge ourselves on our birthdays and wonder, "I am now x years old. Where am I? Who am I? Am I making a difference?"

The universality of such self-doubt is reflected in the *Vidui*, the confessional prayer recited on Yom Kippur, in which we say, "Before I was created I was not worthy (to exist), and now that I am created it is as if I was not created." In other words, when I recite this prayer I realize that, before I was born, the world didn't need me, because if the world needed me, then God would have brought me into the world earlier. I was put into this world precisely when the world needed what I uniquely have to offer. However, now that I exist, am I really fulfilling my purpose for being here? What am I contributing?

These kinds of questions turn birthdays into difficult and challenging days. The older we get, the more our birthday becomes a day for personal assessment and judgment. Similarly, because Rosh Hashanah is the birthday of humanity, there is no better way to celebrate the day than as a time for judgment. It is a time for evaluating ourselves and the progress we have made in fulfilling our purpose and completing our tasks on earth.

THE KINGDOM OF GOD

We are all royal subjects in the kingdom of God. Every one of us has a particular unique job to perform on behalf of the King. Some of us might be street sweepers, some of us might be accountants, some of us might be gardeners. On Rosh Hashanah we are evaluated on our progress in helping to establish the kingdom of God on earth and in taking care of it. And the sentence decreed upon us on that day is only for the purpose of getting us back on track in doing what we have been uniquely created to do.

On Rosh Hashanah we are judged regarding what we did to build and maintain the kingdom this year. However, it is critical to understand that God is not a tyrant or dictator. A tyrant or dictator couldn't care less about his people; he only wants to control them and use them for self-aggrandizement. But God is a King who is dependent on His people, because it is His people who acknowledge His kingship.

God's kingship, his ruling power, is dependent upon us. He has empowered us and entrusted us with building the kingdom that establishes Him as King. His majestic presence on earth is dependent upon our recognition and acceptance of Him as our ruler. Of course, God rules over the world whether we accept that fact or not. The *revelation* of that truth, however, is up to us. If we behave as His royal subjects are meant to behave—and the Torah teaches us exactly how we are to do that—then this world will feel like God's kingdom and will be filled with His majestic presence. But if we deny the power of the

King, then the world will look and feel to us like a wild jungle battered by the impersonal forces of nature.

When I first visited London, I really got the sense that the queen lives there. There is just something about the architecture and overall design of the city that conveys the feeling that this is where Her Majesty Queen Elizabeth resides. Everything appeared so orderly and well maintained. I remember going to Hyde Park and noticing that all the bushes were perfectly trimmed in geometrical shapes. Everybody seemed very formal and on guard. Even the ducks looked like they were on duty. Buckingham Palace, of course, is the city's royal residence. Standing in front of the palace, I saw a fellow wearing a tall furry hat even though it was quite hot. He just stood there, forbidden to speak to tourists. When it came time for the changing of the guard, everything was pomp and circumstance. Not: "Hey guys, it's time to do the change! Come on, let's go!" It was done in a very formal and rigid manner, with every move executed to perfection.

Rosh Hashanah can also feel very formal and rigid. It may be hard to feel spontaneous on that day, because we have such a strong sense that the King is around. Everything has to be sparkling; everything has to be just right.

On Rosh Hashanah we realize that the King is expecting something special from us: He is counting on each and every one of us to establish His kingdom on earth. What an honor and a privilege—each one of us has a special role and a unique way to bring God's presence into this world. We can reveal the King and build His kingdom, or we can destroy the kingdom and exile the

King. And even though, in truth, God will still remain in power, we will not know, see, or feel that, and therefore we will experience ourselves to be living in a vicious jungle. (I explore this idea in greater depth in my book *Seeing God*.) Consequently, on the birthday of humanity we must be extremely careful to evaluate ourselves. We must assess how well we have done our royal job in building and maintaining our world as a Kingdom for God. Did we treat others with the love and respect due a fellow subject and partner? People should be able to walk into our homes, our offices, our shopping malls, look around, and say, "The King must live here . . . this must be the kingdom of the Ultimate, because it is a reflection of the Ultimate."

DON'T MENTION IT

Although earlier I mentioned the *Vidui*, the confessional prayer, Rosh Hashanah is not a day for confessions. The Ari was adamant that we should not mention any wrongdoings on Rosh Hashanah. (We save that for Yom Kippur, which is a day of forgiveness.) When we are in the middle of divine judgment, we do not say anything about our transgressions, because on this day we do not want to make the mistake of becoming preoccupied with ourselves. The *very reason* we make mistakes is that we are often too preoccupied with ourselves, rather than being occupied with how we can help others, how we can establish this earth as God's kingdom, how we can make manifest God's presence in our midst.

Becoming preoccupied with the self is considered a possible destructive consequence of psychoanalysis. When people are turning over every stone in their lives—their childhood, their adolescence, what happened thirty years ago—they can become quite self-absorbed. It is questionable whether such in-depth psychological archeology is actually compatible with Judaism. The Jewish path to self-discovery is to forget yourself, remember others, remember God, and do His will. Doing good and serving the will of God is the most authentic way to affirm your true self—the soul, which is a spark of God. The very reason for most of our mistakes is that we are too self-conscious and self-centered. We are so preoccupied with ourselves that we forget everybody else around us, and we forget God.

A story is told about a frog and a centipede. The frog hated the centipede and constantly tried to trip her up. The centipede, however, moved so fast because of her many legs that the frog could never catch her. One day, the frog came up with a brilliant idea. When he saw the centipede walking down the street, the frog called out, "Hey, Miss Centipede!" The centipede stopped. "Yes?" "I have been wondering for a long time . . . when you walk, which foot do you put first? I see you zooming down the street, and it's just fascinating. I am so impressed. With all those legs, how do you know which foot to put first?" The centipede stopped, scratched her head and responded, "Oh, gee, Mr. Frog, I never thought about it." And from that day on the centipede could never walk again.

Sometimes when we become too self-conscious, we lose touch with the natural wisdom within us that guides us. We can psychoanalyze ourselves to the point of paralysis. We can break ourselves down into so many pieces, while trying so hard to figure ourselves out, that we may end up never able to put ourselves back together again.

Therefore, Rosh Hashanah is not a day for confession; we do not want to become too self-conscious. We are already sufficiently self-conscious on Rosh Hashanah, knowing that this is the Day of Judgment. This is really why we are being judged in the first place—because all of the past year we were too self-conscious and not God-conscious.

There is, however, a fine line between self-awareness and self-consciousness. Those who are totally unaware of themselves have a big problem too. Without self-awareness, you would let people step all over you. You need to have self-respect. You must simply take care not to become too self-conscious and, as a result, self-centered and selfish.

COME BLOW YOUR HORN

The Jewish oral tradition teaches that when we blow the shofar, the King, who is sitting sternly on His throne of judgment, suddenly gets up and takes the seat of compassion (as explained earlier, compassion is the process of kindness overriding justice). The whole nature of the day changes when we blow the shofar. With just one piercing sound, the day is transformed from a day of judgment into a day of compassion. Why? Because by blowing the shofar, we willingly submit ourselves to judgment. And that very act ignites, so to speak, compassion in God.

Nowadays, at the start of a trial, the judge brings the court to order by banging a gavel. But in the olden days, a Jewish trial began with a blast of a shofar.

Now imagine you are summoned to stand trial before the King in order to be judged for your deeds during the entire last year. Inside, you are trembling, frightened, overwhelmed. Nonetheless, you bravely walk up to the judge's desk, grab the shofar lying there, and blow it. Everyone is absolutely shocked. You not only don't evade the trial or deny the charges, you actually invite the judgment, announcing to all present, "This is my day of judgment. I want no delay. Go ahead, judge me now."

When we blow the shofar, we initiate the judgment. We are saying that we want to be judged and we are not in the least afraid of the outcome. We joyfully accept the judgment and embrace it with love. How could this be?

Most people are either in denial of judgment or spend much effort evading it. On January 1, when a large part of the world celebrates New Year's Day, many people subject themselves to a personal evaluation, resolving to improve in the coming year. However, New Year's has also become a time to get drunk. People make resolutions and then get smashed. I can understand why. Judgment, even self-imposed judgment, is painful, frightening, and challenging. It is natural to just want to get drunk, to run away and deny it.

The book of Psalms teaches, "Happy are those who know the secret of the blast of the shofar." What is the secret? Can't anybody figure out how to blow a shofar?

The real secret of blowing the shofar is knowing that when you lovingly accept and embrace judgment, it is automatically transformed into compassion. This is because you realize that the one who is judging you is not only your King but also your Father, as the saying goes in Hebrew: *Avinu Malkeinu,* "our Father is our King." He is not judging you because He is insulted by your behavior, or because you get on His nerves, or because He wants to get back at you and slap you. He is judging you because He loves you and cares about you.

When you don't understand who is judging you and why, then you will naturally run from it. But when you understand that your Father is the Judge, and all He wants is the best for you, then you will lovingly embrace a day of judgment as an opportunity for change and growth.

If we deny our mistakes and avoid paying the consequences, then we continue to make them and continue to hurt ourselves. Most of us would sincerely prefer to live in reality rather than deny it and live an illusion. But despite our best intentions, we often lose our way. When we transgress the mitzvot, we forfeit our mission to build God's kingdom on earth, and we cause harm to ourselves. Our neglecting to obey God's will becomes the source of our own personal destruction.

Therefore, we tremble with joy on Rosh Hashanah, because we joyously accept God's judgment. We understand its true meaning, and we know that the Judge is our Father and our King and He loves us. We know that no matter how harsh may be the sentence that He decrees upon us, it is exactly what we need to get back on track in order to fulfill our life's mission.

As noted earlier, Carl Jung once said that neurosis is a substitute for legitimate suffering. In other words, when we deny our suffering, we end up suffering in other ways and causing ourselves more harm. I would say that the same principle applies when we avoid judgment and are not willing to accept the consequences of our behavior. When we do that, we continue to hold on to the illusion that we are self-defined beings, existing independent of God. This attitude generates feelings of alienation from the true source, context, and essence of our very soul. The feeling of alienation from God, who is the source of all life and all pleasure, is the cause of all pain and sickness, both physical and spiritual.

When we accept God's judgment, then we no longer need it. The very acceptance of the judgment fixes the cause of all our mistakes and transgressions, because we realize that we are not independent of God and not unaccountable to Him. God does not need to decree upon us any corrective consequences to get us back on track, because when we lovingly accept His judgment, we put ourselves back on track. By doing so, we show we have learned our lesson. Therefore, the Judge immediately gets up from His throne of judgment and takes the seat of compassion.

But if we run away from judgment, then what we are really doing is refusing to let go of the illusion of our independence, and we are refusing to accept that God is the Judge and King.

ECHOES OF THE FIRST SHOFAR

The Torah tells us that God asked Abraham to sacrifice his son Isaac. Abraham's love for and devotion to God were so great that he chose to fulfill God's request. However, just when Abraham was about to perform this unbelievable act of faith, God stopped him and told him to sacrifice a ram instead.

The Midrash tells us that, after this event, Abraham said to God, "God, You know and I know that when You asked me to sacrifice my son, I had every right to say no to You from the standpoint of justice, but I said yes. I was willing to pass on my rights and override justice to do as You asked. Now I am asking the same of You. In the future, my descendants will be standing on Rosh Hashanah and they will be asking You for forgiveness. From the standpoint of justice, You will have every right to say no to them, but when You hear them blow the ram's horn, the shofar, then remember the time I had the right to say no to You and yet nonetheless I said yes."

With Abraham's merit weighing the scales of justice in our favor, we have nothing to fear.

And thus on Rosh Hashanah we celebrate our accountability to God, the Judge, because we know that He is actually our loving Parent who loves us unconditionally. Knowing this truth gives us the courage to lovingly accept His judgment, so that we can get back on track and dedicate ourselves to loving God and our fellow subjects with whom we share this splendid kingdom of divine love.

—FIVE—

Yom Kippur

Celebrating Forgiveness

Rosh Hashanah and Yom Kippur are very different experiences. Rosh Hashanah is the Day of Judgment. God is judging me, and judgment can make me feel distant from the Judge. In fact, the Hebrew word for a judicial decree is *gezer*, from the verb *li'gzor*, meaning "to cut." That is what judgment can do. It can make me feel cut off from the Judge.

In addition to being the Day of Judgment, Rosh Hashanah is a day to acknowledge the truth of monotheism. It's the day on which I recognize that God is the one and only King, and I am not the King. There is an infinite gap that separates the King and myself. Next to the

Infinite, I am infinitesimal. This past year I did wrong and disobeyed the King's will, because I mistakenly thought that I knew better than God and that what I wanted to do would bring me more success and pleasure than what God asked of me. But now, on Rosh Hashanah, I realize how foolish I was to think this way. I realize that my true fulfillment can only come from obeying God—the one and only King who created me and this world.

Rosh Hashanah is a day of intense fear, reverence, and awe. We fear the consequences of our wrongdoings and realize that, in order to repair the damage we have caused ourselves and others, we may have to suffer very difficult and painful times. We feel reverence on this day because we are acutely conscious that God is the King, the Ultimate Authority, and the Mastermind of the Universe. We recognize how feeble our minds are in comparison to the greatness of His wisdom. We realize how foolish we were to reject His guidance and rebel against His directions. And we are awestruck by the fact that, next to God's perfection, we are truly minuscule and incomplete. Each of us is less than a drop of water in the oceans that fill the earth. How could we have even thought to do other than God's will?

And finally, on Rosh Hashanah, we recognize that God's judgment comes from His love for us, and when we accept it, it is transformed into compassion. However, even while we rejoice in our trembling, we tremble nonetheless.

Yom Kippur, however, is another story. Yom Kippur is the Day of Atonement, which is defined by love and forgiveness. On Yom Kippur we get a glimpse of ourselves, our choices, and our relationship to God from another perspective—God's perspective—and come to recognize how inseparably close we are to God. This is the transformative power of Yom Kippur.

There is a cryptic verse in the book of Psalms: "The days were formed, and one of them is His." Our sages say this day is Yom Kippur. There is one day—God's day—when we get a glimpse of the way the world looks from His perspective and everything changes in how we see ourselves. On Yom Kippur we see our lives from the perspective of the World to Come, where we'll get to see the whole picture.

The Talmud teaches that in this world, when something good happens to us, we praise God: "Blessed is He who is good and does good." But when something bad happens, we must say, "Blessed is He who is a true Judge." However, in the future we will say, "Blessed is He who is good and does good" even about the misfortunes in our lives. In other words, when we will look back and see the whole picture, we will realize that every bad thing that happened to us contributed to God's plan, which is to bring upon us ultimate goodness. This is also true about every bad thing that we *did*.

According to the Kabbalah, although we have the free choice to do other than God's will, God is always in control. In other words, even when we can do other than God's will, we cannot *oppose* His will or undermine His plan. Therefore, when we have done wrong and are sorry for that, we must realize that no matter what we have done, it can all be recycled back into God's plan and contribute to the ultimate good of the world. Of course, this does not mean that we can just go ahead and do wrong. The path of transgression removes us from God. This distance causes us feelings of alienation and spiritual anguish, which may become manifest as physical ailments.

However, it is important to remember that if we sincerely regret our wrongdoings and resolve never to do them again, then we are forgiven and our past will be recycled and put toward future good.

Yom Kippur is an amazing day of transformation when our darkest deeds from the past turn into light. This is because the light of the World to Come, so to speak, is shining into our world on this day. We can receive this light and be transformed by it if we connect with the expanded consciousness of Yom Kippur through the proper acts, prayers, and thoughts prescribed for the day.

Rosh Hashanah is a day dedicated to understanding ourselves and God in the light of monotheism. Yom Kippur, however, celebrates how everything looks in the light of panentheism, which is the perspective of the World to Come.

Monotheism means that there is one God, one King, and we are not God. Panentheism (which should not be confused with pantheism) teaches that God is not just the one and only ruling power and there are no other gods, but that God is absolutely the one and only reality—there is nothing but God, and we exist within God. That does not mean that you and I are the Almighty. However, we are souls—sparks, aspects, and expressions of the Almighty. We do not exist apart from God; rather, we exist within Him.

As the Kabbalah explains, in the beginning of Genesis, God created a space within Himself, so to speak, and within that space, He created beings other than Himself. This self-imposed limitation is called *tzimtzum*, the constriction or withdrawal of divinity. God withdrew and limited His endless being to create a space and a place for beings other than Himself—free beings who can do other than His will.

We exist within God much as an idea exists within the mind of the thinker. The difference, however, is that an idea has no free choice. We have free choice but, mysteriously, any choice we make still remains within the context of God's being and the confines of God's will. Therefore, we are free and yet, ironically, God is still absolutely in control. We are free to disobey and do other than God's will, but we are not able to oppose God's will or undermine His plan. This, of course, is a paradox that cannot be comprehended by our rational minds.

What difference, then, do our choices make?

Our real choice is whether to become a conscious partner with God in the making of history or an unconscious tool in His plan. We can choose to do God's will and contribute to His plan in an active, conscious way and thereby experience the ecstasy of the unchangeable truth that God is one and we are one with God. Or we can choose to oppose God's will and, ironically, through our own choices, fulfill God's plan without even knowing it. When we do this, however, we deny ourselves the joyous knowledge of our inseparable connection to God and instead suffer pains of alienation and separation from God.

We choose to disobey God's will only when we mistakenly think that we exist as separate from and independent of God. When we do that, we support and nurture illusions about ourselves. The truth is that our wrongdoings are actually our punishment. They make us feel disconnected, alienated, and isolated from God, who is actually the ground, context, and essence of our very existence. In other words, our choices create our own heaven or hell.

If we knew deep in our hearts that God is one and that we are one with God, then even though we could do other than God's will, we would not want to.

THE SCAPEGOAT

When the Temple in Jerusalem still stood, a strange sacrificial service was performed on Yom Kippur that today seems to us the very antithesis of Judaism. Two identical goats were brought before the High Priest and lots were drawn. One goat was designated for God and the other for the *Azazel*—the satanic force. The High Priest would confess the wrongdoings of the people, symbolically place all their transgressions upon the goat destined for *Azazel*, and send it off into the wilderness.

If this were done on any other day of the year it would constitute idolatry. But on Yom Kippur even the darkest act can be transformed into light. On Yom Kippur even an act that is the antithesis of Judaism, can, from

God's perspective, actually contribute to God's plan. Even though during the year this act would promote and nurture the illusion that we exist independent of and separate from God, on Yom Kippur it ultimately contributes to the higher consciousness that we are one with God. Perhaps this is why it is called the Day of At-one-ment.

Strangely, the name "Yom Kippur" hints that it is a day like Purim. (*Yom* means "day," the prefix *k* means "like," and *purim* means "lots," which were also drawn on Purim.) That is because the mysterious truth revealed on Yom Kippur—that we exist within God—is revealed with even greater intensity and clarity on the holiday of Purim.

On Purim we are supposed to drink until we are so drunk that we confuse "blessed be Mordechai" (the hero of the Purim story) and "cursed be Haman" (its villain). In other words, we are so intoxicated that we can't tell the difference between Mordechai, the heroic leader of the Jewish people, and Haman, the evil person, who tried to destroy them. How could this be?

On Purim we are able to say "blessed is Haman" because although he was evil, even Haman contributed to God's plan for goodness. (How so? See chapter 9.)

Yom Kippur is like Purim because on that day even our misdeeds can be seen as positive forces in serving God's will and plan. Therefore, on Yom Kippur God forgives us and we can forgive ourselves. The darkness can serve the light, and the ugly past can be recycled into a beautiful future.

THE JOY OF REGRET

On Yom Kippur you can confess all your transgressions to God with the realization that they too can contribute to His plan. On Yom Kippur, when God's oneness is so manifest, the mention of your transgressions can be a source of greater light. On Yom Kippur, when God's oneness is so revealed and the light of His eternal love for us is shining, you don't need to be afraid or ashamed like on Rosh Hashanah, the Day of Judgment. Confess your transgressions even a million times. In fact, it's good to be as clear and precise as you can, because on Yom Kippur you actually experience greater love precisely from every single wrong you regret you did.

Moments of love are the best times to remember when we wronged each other, because when we feel so at one with each other we are able to appreciate how the conflict of the past actually served to enhance our unity. In a funny way, conflicts are great for relationships. Once the storm calms and we stop yelling at each other, we suddenly feel so foolish; we then uncontrollably embrace and profusely apologize. In the back of our minds, however, there is a very strange sense of satisfaction that this was a great fight. The conflict, alienation, and separation that it created actually contributed to a heightened awareness of our true love and eternal oneness.

The best time to remember our mistakes and wrongdoings and ask forgiveness of our beloved is in moments of love. The contrast between the bad times that were and the good time that is happening right now generates even greater feelings of love and appreciation. Therefore, the dark conflicts of the past, when viewed in the present light of love, actually serve to intensify the brilliance and warmth of the moment.

Yom Kippur, however, is more than a *moment* of love—it is a full day. And it reveals the truth that God's love forever shines upon us. It is only our foolish attitudes and wrongdoings that have blocked out the light, creating the dark shadows in our life. As the prophet Isaiah said in the name of God, "It is only your wrongdoing that separates you and Me." In other words, it is our misdeeds that cause us to feel that we and God are separate. But that is untrue. We are forever one with God, and there is nothing that we can do to change that fact, although there is much that we can do to *conceal* that fact.

On Yom Kippur the timeless truth of God's oneness—and humanity's oneness with God—is bright and clear. So on Yom Kippur, let yourself go. Remember every dumb, wrong thing you ever did that seemed to separate you from God, because on Yom Kippur this only adds to the ecstasy of love and the joy of forgiveness. On Yom Kippur the dark illusion of separateness enhances the incredible light of your oneness with God. God allows you to make mistakes and do wrong, because He knows that eventually the painful feelings of alienation will increase and enhance the ecstasy of your love.

I have heard it explained that the first couple, Adam and Eve, ate of the forbidden fruit because they wanted to increase their awareness of God's oneness and their closeness with God by creating a contrast to it—

separateness. It was a noble attempt, but it got them (and all of humanity) into terrible trouble. This is why the Talmud teaches that you should never think, "I will transgress, so that I can later apologize (and feel even closer to God as a result)," just as you can't say, "I will start a fight with my spouse so that we can make up later and better appreciate how much we really love each other." It just doesn't work that way. But don't worry, plenty of opportunities present themselves for fights with your spouse—you don't have to create them. And there are plenty of times that you will transgress, without any need for planning. But when conflict and breakdowns happen, it's good to know that even the fight can be used to enhance your love.

On Yom Kippur we can find the blessing in all our evil deeds and wrongdoings. This, of course, is true only if we sincerely regret what we've done and commit that we will never return to those foolish ways again. Only then can we appreciate that everything we did that took us so far away from God is now helping to revitalize and increase our feelings of closeness and love for God. If we realize that, then all the conflict was worth it. The past is redeemed in that moment. And then all the pain of the past turns into ecstatic pleasure.

When you fight with your spouse, one reason to make up is fear. You fear that she will tell all your friends what a jerk you are, or he will lock you out of the house. Therefore, to save yourself the discomfort, you say you are sorry. However, there is another, higher reason to make up: you could apologize for the sake of love. You realize how silly it is to fight with the one you love, the one with whom you are one. For a moment you lost your mind and forgot how much you really care for this person and how deep and eternal is your connection. The issue of contention was so petty compared to the power and beauty of your soul connection to each other.

When you apologize because you fear punishment, you successfully end the argument and prevent further damage. But you don't cash in on your conflict—the fight was simply a waste of energy, and this is really just a ceasefire. But when love motivates you, then the conflict turns into a force that promotes an even greater awareness of your oneness and adds to your love. Then, you actually gain.

So it is when we fight with God, so to speak, as when we transgress His commandments and turn against His will. Turning away from God causes separation and alienation and is the opposite of a mitzvah, the purpose of which is to promote God's oneness and our oneness with God—to reveal the light of love. But when separateness is recycled to promote oneness, then really what you have is a mitzvah.

However, this conversion of a wrong into a right, into a mitzvah, can happen only when our return to God is motivated by our love for God and our desire to experience God's oneness and our oneness with Him. Return to God motivated by fear of punishment does not accomplish this transformation. Return out of fear still comes from a perspective that we exist separately from and independently of God—that we are here on earth and God is over there in heaven—but that we should not act against God's will for fear of punishment. Return from fear cancels out the negative effects of wrongdoing, but it cannot transform it into the positive force of a mitzvah like return from love, which empowers us to cash in on our previous debts.

Yom Kippur is cash-in day. It offers the perfect ambience to return to God in love, redeem our dark past, and turn it into light.

ALOUD AND PROUD

During the year when we recite the Shema, the Jewish testimony of God's oneness, *Shema Israel*, YHVH *Eloheinu*, YHVH *ehad*, "Hear O Israel, the Lord is our God, the Lord is One," we say it out loud, but the following verse, "Blessed be the name of His glorious kingdom for all eternity," we whisper. On Yom Kippur, however, we also recite this second verse out loud. Why?

The *Zohar* explains that the first declaration is the higher testimony of God's oneness, while the second is a lower testimony of God's oneness. The Talmud adds that the second declaration is really not befitting, but due to our current low spiritual level, we need to say it. Therefore, we do it in a whisper.

The Shema captures the meaning of panentheism, expressing that God is absolutely one and only—there is nothing besides God; all exists within God. The statement that follows—"Blessed be the name of His glorious kingdom for all eternity"—expresses the monotheistic perspective, which holds that God is like a king and we have no other kings. This statement does not communicate the highest awareness of God's true oneness. In fact, it could actually be seen as promoting the illusion that we exist as separate from and independent of God. The perspective of monotheism, however, is a necessary step toward the full understanding of God's oneness that includes all that exists. Therefore, we must say it, but we say it softly because we are not proud of the fact that we have not yet reached the ultimate recognition of God's true oneness that encompasses us. On Yom Kippur, however, when the light of panentheism is shining bright, we can appreciate—and proudly acclaim—that even the illusion of our separate existence from God now enhances the truth. (This is similar to the idea that on this day we can confess our transgressions and turn them into positive forces.)

Although in some ways monotheism supports and promotes the painful feeling of our independence and separateness from God, it is an essential preparation toward the ideal awareness of panentheism. Judaism first teaches us the perspective of monotheism before it reveals the truth of panentheism. This is because we first need to internalize the truth that we are distinct from and other than God. If we were exposed to panentheism before we were well acquainted with monotheism, we might mistakenly think that we are God and that all is God. In truth, we are one with God, but we are not God. We are *other* than God, but paradoxically, we are one with God because we exist *within* God.

During the year, we do not want to announce our monotheistic beliefs too loudly. We are not especially proud of the fact that we need monotheism to protect us from confusing panentheism with pantheism. But on Yom Kippur we can loudly proclaim what we believe, because on this day we are able to recognize that even the feelings of separateness now promote and enhance our awareness of God's true oneness and our oneness with God. The light is enhanced by its contrast with the darkness.

PURIFYING WATERS

About Yom Kippur, the Torah tells us that "the very day atones." In fact, there are certain categories of transgressions that are atoned for only on Yom Kippur.

Let's say you committed one of those offenses, but you regretted what you did. You decided, "I don't want to do this again. I am sorry that I did it. And I promise that I will never do it again." Even though this constitutes true regret, atonement and reparation happen only on Yom Kippur. There's something metaphysical about the day of Yom Kippur that purifies and rectifies the past. There are certain transgressions that cannot be completely fixed or atoned for until you step into the day of Yom Kippur.

Yom Kippur is a *mikvah* in time. When you immerse yourself in a *mikvah*—a purifying ritual bath—there can be absolutely nothing between your skin and the water, according to Jewish law. Before immersion in the *mikvah*, you have to scrutinize yourself to ensure that nothing at all separates you from the *mikvah* waters. Even if you have a loose hair sticking to your skin, the immersion is not considered total. This is because the waters of the *mikvah* represent the oneness of God. When you enter a *mikvah*, you are immersing yourself back into God's all-encompassing oneness, simulating the experience of existing within God. For this to work, there must be absolutely no separation between you and God.

In the *mikvah*, you are one with its waters, completely absorbed, submerged, and surrounded. By immersing your body in the *mikvah*, you express your desire to merge your soul back into the oneness of God and acknowledge that nothing at all separates you from Him. Thus, you become pure again—physically and spiritually.

The status of impurity is simply the manifestation of our separateness from God caused by our wrongdoings. We wouldn't choose to do other than God's will unless we were under the illusion that we exist as separate from and independent of Him. This attitude, and the choices we make based on it, create the spiritual status called *tumah*, "impurity." On the other hand, *tahara*, "purity," is about dissolving that separation and returning to the awareness of God's oneness and our oneness with God. We can achieve this state of purity through the *mikvah*.

On Rosh Hashanah God is perceived as if He is over there and we are over here. God is the King, and we are neither God nor King. God is the Judge, and we are the judged. We feel fear, and we feel far. However, on Yom Kippur God is our place, space, context, and essence. Even though we recognize that we and God are clearly not one and the same, we are completely one with God. He is our *mikvah* and not even a hair separates us. On Yom Kippur we know that God is one and we exist within God, completely absorbed, submerged, and surrounded by His being. We feel close, and we feel loved.

It is customary on the day before Yom Kippur to immerse oneself in a *mikvah* in preparation for experiencing the day as a *mikvah* in time, when we can truly experience how we are actually always immersed in God.

THE HOLY OF HOLIES

Yom Kippur is the only day of the year when the High Priest, while performing the sacrificial service, entered the innermost chamber in the Temple. This chamber was called the Holy of Holies (the one holy that includes the many holies) because the truth of God's oneness—the One who includes the many—was manifest there.

The High Priest had to be completely pure when he walked into that chamber. If he was physically or spiritually impure (if he thought and acted as if he were an independent, self-contained being, existing separate from God), then he immediately died upon entering the Holy of Holies. The truth revealed in the Holy of Holies would simply obliterate his false premise of independent, separate existence, causing his death.

If, however, he safely entered the Holy of Holies, he then pronounced the name of God YHVH (the Tetragrammaton), which is forbidden to anyone else at any other time. The entire Temple would then be filled with the truth of God's all-inclusive oneness. The massive crowd of people tightly packed into the Temple then bowed down, and each person miraculously had plenty of space to do so. In other words, the truth of God's oneness manifest on Yom Kippur transcended the limits of space and revealed how the one can hold the many.

That the one can hold the many is an astonishing truth that we have since forgotten.

The Baal Shem Tov, the eighteenth-century founder of the Hasidic movement, was once traveling in a wagon that was packed full with passengers. Even though there was no room to move, when he saw a hitchhiker on the road, he nonetheless urged the driver to stop and offer the fellow a ride. "But there's no more room for anybody else," responded the driver. "What are you talking about?" said the Baal Shem Tov. "All we need to do is love each other just a little bit more, and there will be plenty of room."

God's oneness is the miraculous power of love. It transcends the limits of time and space. It includes everyone and everything within it.

THE FAST TRACK TO ONENESS

The Talmud teaches that in the World to Come we will neither eat nor drink; we will simply be satiated by our feelings of closeness to God. On Yom Kippur—because we are basking in the light of the World to Come—we too are satiated by our intimate connection with God. This is the deeper reason that we don't eat on this day.

When the light of God's oneness is shining, we do not want our bodies to create shadows. It is the body that promotes the illusion that we exist as independent and separate from God; it suggests that we exist in this sack of skin separate from the rest of existence. Therefore, we fast. We do not feed our bodies, nor do we even relate to our bodies on Yom Kippur. We abstain from all bodily pleasures: sexual relations, washing, or applying any types of lotions or creams.

We also don't wear leather shoes on this day. Today not wearing leather shoes on Yom Kippur is not about giving up luxury or comfort, because there are also non-leather shoes that are just as expensive and comfortable. The point is that leather shoes, made from animal hides, represent the body, which we do not want to relate to on Yom Kippur.

When Moses approached the Burning Bush, God told him to take off his shoes, which also metaphorically meant to take off his body. The shoe is to the body as the body is to the soul. Not wearing leather shoes on Yom Kippur is an external act that reflects an internal state of being. On Yom Kippur we disassociate ourselves, for one day, from our bodies so that they do not separate us from immersing ourselves in the *mikvah* of God's oneness. In this way, we acknowledge that we exist within God. We say: "I am one with Him, and I am loved by Him with the very love that He loves Himself, because I am an aspect of His very self."

SATAN'S DAY OFF

The Talmudic sages teach us that on Yom Kippur Satan takes the day off.

According to Jewish tradition, Satan is not a red devil with horns and a pitchfork who works against God. Satan is a force in the universe created by God. Satan's purpose is to challenge us, so that we can rise to higher levels of awareness of our connection to God.

This idea is expressed in the Garden of Eden story. God created the evil snake and sent him on a holy mission in the Garden of Eden to tempt Adam and Eve to do other than His will—to think that they existed as separate from and independent of God. This, of course, was really an opportunity for them to become fully conscious of God's true oneness and their oneness with God and to experience the ecstasy of love. (As we know, they blew it, but the snake was only doing his job. Had they succeeded, the snake would not be seen by us today as the villain of the story, merely as the catalyst to a happy ending.)

The *Zohar* metaphorically describes evil in the world as a prostitute who has been hired by the king (God) to seduce his son the prince (us). Of course the king does not want her to succeed. However, he wants to create an opportunity for the prince to realize his own royal integrity by resisting this great temptation and choosing to act in the way that befits his nobility. Until he passes the test, the son's royal status is merely an inherited title and a wardrobe of regal clothing but not the genuine expression of himself, accomplished through the power of his own choices and determined efforts.

So this is the role of Satan. But on Yom Kippur he takes the day off, because he knows that, from the perspective of the World to Come, all his efforts to separate us from God only become the very glue that connects us to God with even greater consciousness.

On Yom Kippur we send Satan the *Azazel* offering to show our appreciation. Although this would generally be considered idolatry, a transgression separating us from God, on Yom Kippur it is a mitzvah; from the perspective of the World to Come, the powers that promote separateness from God are actually serving to increase the ultimate revelation of God's oneness and love. This again is similar to Purim when we bless the evil Haman. We bless and thank the forces of evil, because we now realize in retrospect that all the separateness Satan has caused us to suffer actually enhances our experience of God's oneness and our oneness with God.

In summary, Yom Kippur is a *mikvah* in time. It is a day when we can immerse ourselves in the all-embracing oneness of God and emerge pure. On that day the light of the World to Come shines into the world, and we can see ourselves and our actions from God's perspective. In that light, even our transgressions of the past become blessings for our future, the darkness now serves to enhance the light, and the ugly conflicts now increase the splendor and beauty of the love we share with God.

On Yom Kippur we celebrate forgiveness, because we realize that only love is real—everything else is illusion.

SIX

Sukkot and Simchat Torah

Celebrating Wholeness, Spontaneity, and Anticipation

Four days after Yom Kippur, we celebrate the seven-day-long festival called Sukkot ("Booths"), which is immediately followed by an eighth day of celebration known in Israel as both Shemini Atzeret ("Eighth Day of Assembly") and Simchat Torah ("Joy of the Torah"), though in the Diaspora this celebration stretches to the eighth and ninth days.

In preparation for this festival, we build a sukkah, which is a temporary booth covered by a roof made of *sechach*—palm fronds, tree branches, or any other plant material that is detached from the ground. There must be enough *sechach* to provide shade, but it must not be so densely packed that we cannot see the stars at night. During the entire week of the holiday, we are required to leave our permanent homes and take up residence in the sukkah. We eat our meals there, entertain our guests there, and even sleep there. The sukkah reminds us of the huts that the Israelites lived in during the forty years that they wandered in the desert, prior to finally entering the land of Israel. The sukkah also symbolizes the miraculous clouds of glory that hovered over them, giving them shelter and protection.

Another main feature of the holiday is "the four species" which are bound together and waved: the palm branch, three myrtle branches, two willow branches, and a citron (which looks somewhat like a lemon). We are commanded to own a set of these four species, and each day wave it toward the four corners of the world, as well as upward and downward.

RECOVERING OUR INNER CHILD

We just spent ten intense days—from Rosh Hashanah to Yom Kippur—immersed in intensive introspection, probing the depth of our souls to uncover our flaws and confront our mistakes, expressing heartfelt remorse for our wrongdoings and courageously committing ourselves to make lasting changes. Then, the very next day after Yom Kippur, we are out and about like playful children admiring the beauty of nature, looking at palm branches, willows, and myrtles. And we are building and decorating a clubhouse—the sukkah. What's going on?

Although we value the maturity of High Holiday observance, we pay a price for the process. The concentration and intensity of the last ten days have weakened us and damaged the spontaneity and joy of our inner child. And although we've just completed a process of spiritual healing, there are side effects that need to be attended to. Even though we are over the sickness, we still need to become healthy, whole, and strong again. We need to reconnect with our life force. On Sukkot we recover our playfulness and our zest for life.

Passover is referred to in the holiday prayers as the "time of our freedom." Shavuot is called "the time of the giving of our Torah." But Sukkot is described as the "time of our happiness." On Sukkot we reclaim the joy and liveliness of our inner child and remember, "Toyrah 'R' Us."

HAPPY DAYS ARE HERE AGAIN

Another reason Sukkot is called the "time of our happiness" is that it celebrates our successful completion of the arduous journey that began on Rosh Hashanah. There is much to rejoice over when you feel you have a new lease on life after finally completing the challenging process that began with judgment and continued through regret and resolution to forgiveness. This process is similar to that of a husband and wife who violated their loving relationship with harsh words and hurtful acts. Ironically, at the end of their journey—from disillusionment and judgment, through regret and resolve, to apologies and forgiveness—there is great love and joy. In fact, the hard times and the upheaval in their relationship and its final resolution generated even greater feelings of love and happiness than before the problems began.

So too Sukkot celebrates the joyous relief and ecstatic love that naturally follows the distance and alienation from God caused by our transgressions, the acceptance of the judgment of Rosh Hashanah, and the forgiveness of Yom Kippur.

On Rosh Hashanah we experience God as a Judge. On Yom Kippur we experience God as a forgiving Parent. But on Sukkot we celebrate God as our Lover. According to the Kabbalah, when we sit in the close confines of the sukkah, we feel God hugging us.

WHOLE IN ONE

Judaism teaches that the goal of life and the source of true happiness is holiness. We are holy when we are whole—integrated and harmonious with our inner self, with our nation, with the rest of humanity, with nature, and with God. We accomplish this by fulfilling the commandments of God.

When we violate God's commandments, we undermine our holiness; we disintegrate and become at odds with our inner self, our nation, humanity, nature, and God. In other words, when we go against the will of God, we estrange ourselves from the Soul of Souls, the Ultimate Self—God—and therefore also from our inner self, which is a spark of God. We set ourselves apart from the Jewish people (our collective national self), and we alienate ourselves from the rest of humanity, because we neglect our responsibility to the world. Because we are not fulfilling our divine purpose on earth, nature resists supporting us and dis-ease increases in the world.

From Rosh Hashanah until Yom Kippur, we work our way back from disintegration to wholeness and happiness. On Sukkot we reach the finish line and celebrate becoming whole again. As part of this celebration of wholeness, we take the four species and wave them toward the four corners of the world, as well as up and down.

The Talmudic sages tell us that the four species represent different parts of ourselves. The citron symbolizes our heart; the palm branch symbolizes our spine; the shape of the myrtle leaves suggests our eyes; and the willow leaves look like our mouth. Therefore, when we hold them together to fulfill the commandment of waving them on Sukkot, it is as if we are pulling ourselves together and dedicating ourselves to God.

The four species also symbolize the different kinds of Jews that make up a community. The citron has taste and fragrance—representing Jews who are both learned in Torah and also do good deeds. The palm frond comes from a date tree, which has taste but no fragrance; it represents Torah learning without good deeds. The myrtle has fragrance but no taste, alluding to those who do good deeds but are not learned. And finally the willow, with neither taste nor fragrance, stands for Jews who are un-learned and do no good. But each contributes something to the whole.

Therefore, when you hold the four species together, you are not only expressing the wholeness within your-self, you are also acknowledging that you are connected with the whole nation of Israel, all your fellow Jews, no matter who they are. You then wave the four species toward the four corners of the world as well as up and down, to show that the whole world, all of humanity, heaven above and the earth below, all belong to God.

Wholeness is a theme of Sukkot. Indeed, the com-mandment to live in the sukkah is a celebration of our return to wholeness.

Although there are specific requirements as to the height of a sukkah, there are no limits as to how wide and long it can be. In fact, the Talmud says that it can be big enough to accommodate the entire Jewish people. In other words, the sukkah expresses the peace and wholeness that we can share with every Jew in the world—those who are alive today and those who came before us.

It is customary each day of the holiday, just before we begin a festive meal in our sukkah, to symbolically invite the *ushpizin* as our dinner guests. The *ushpizin* are the souls of the ancient founders, visionaries, and leaders of the Jewish people: Abraham, Isaac, Jacob, Moses, Aaron, Joseph, and David. This custom celebrates the truth that on Sukkot we again feel one with the entire Jewish people, not only of our time but of all time. When we do wrong and violate the teachings of the Torah, we break our link to Jewish history and forfeit our part in their destiny. However, on Sukkot, now that we have completed our return to God and His Torah, we experience ourselves as reunited with the collective soul of the Jewish people, including those great souls who were our ancestors and pathfinders.

BACK TO NATURE

We are now ready to return to nature, and nature supports us in our holy efforts. Therefore, we embrace the four species and in turn feel embraced by the natural setting of the sukkah, shaded during the day by its roof made of foliage and watching the stars overhead as we go to sleep at night. In fact, according to the Kabbalah, the sukkah has the ambience of the Garden of Eden, where humanity lived in complete harmony with nature and where all our physical needs were naturally provided for without "the sweat of our brow."

Some sages explain that the sukkah even has the ambience of the World to Come. Even though on Yom Kippur we got a glimpse of the World to Come, to get that glimpse we had to leave this world by fasting and abstaining from other physical pleasures. However, on Sukkot—now that we have already purified ourselves of our wrongdoings—we can experience heaven on earth by feasting in our sukkah, experiencing the World to Come in this world precisely through physical pleasure. The fasting on Yom Kippur prepares us for the feasting on Sukkot. Abstaining from the physical pleasures of this world on Yom Kippur is only meant to heal us from the sickness of overindulgence. But, once we take control of ourselves and free ourselves from our transgressions, addictions, and obsessions, we are free to enjoy the pleasures of this world on Sukkot.

On Yom Kippur we leave this world and experience union with God by transcending nature and abstaining from physical pleasures. However, on Sukkot we experience union with God through nature and through physical pleasures. This is the journey of holiness.

When we experience no conflict between the physical and the spiritual, the natural and the supernatural, the eternal and the temporal, then we experience the epitome of holiness. We enjoy perfect harmony, synergy, and wholeness.

This truth is clearly expressed in the commandment to dwell in the sukkah. It is one of the very few commandments that we fulfill using our entire bodies—by living, eating, drinking, conversing, and sleeping in the sukkah. After the hard work of the High Holidays, we can now relax and experience the immersion of our everyday natural life in God's all-embracing presence. The sukkah teaches us that we are completely one with God even when we are tending to such mundane needs as eating and sleeping. Our choice is to realize this truth and celebrate it.

Sukkot is the celebration of ultimate holiness. We feel the ecstatic joy of being integrated within ourselves, one with our people and our ancestors throughout time, renewed in our commitment to humanity, and harmonized with nature. We are thrilled to know and feel that we have finally returned to our true selves. We are whole in One—whole *with* God and whole *in* God.

OFF TO A RIGHT START

As mentioned earlier, the holiday of Sukkot reminds us of the huts of the Israelites as they wandered for forty years in the desert after their miraculous Exodus from Egypt. It would stand to reason then that Sukkot should be celebrated right after the holiday of Passover. However, the Talmudic sages explain that since Passover is in the spring, living in the sukkah at that time of year would not be anything special. It is common to be outside during the warm months of the year. After Yom Kippur, however, when it starts to get cold, people generally take shelter inside. We go outside only because God commands us to.

Leaving our homes precisely when we are not naturally inclined to do so internalizes another one of the important lessons of Sukkot: God is our only true shelter, and we must trust in Him. We often transgress the will of God because we mistakenly think we know what is best for us, rather than trusting in God. This was the mistake that Adam and Eve made when they ate of the forbidden fruit. They thought they knew better than God as to what would best serve their interests and accomplish their life goals. Trusting God is a vital truth to internalize especially after the High Holiday season, just before we return to the challenges of our everyday lives.

There is another advantage to celebrating Sukkot at the start of autumn rather than after Passover in the spring. Autumn is the season of the harvest, which is the time when we are subject to the tricks of the ego. It is too easy, after reaping the fruits of our labor, to take pride in our accomplishment. Pride and ego make for fertile ground in which the seeds of evil can grow; they were the two reasons Adam and Eve disobeyed the will of God. Sensing the godliness within themselves, they aspired to become all-powerful and all-knowing, just like God. Therefore, they were easily seduced by the snake's claim that the fruit of the Tree of Knowledge would empower them to become gods and allow them to determine for themselves what is good or bad.

Therefore, on Sukkot, as we step into the new year, we protect ourselves from returning to our wrongdoings of the past year by embracing the message of the sukkah—in God we trust and before Him we are humbled.

INNER PEACE

In addition to living in the sukkah and waving the four species, it is customary on Sukkot to read the book of Ecclesiastes, written by King Solomon. The Talmudic sages tell us that King Solomon was inspired to write this book when he realized that the Temple that he built would be destroyed in the future. Lamenting over that excruciating truth, he wrote, "Futility of futilities, of what worth is the work of man under the sun."

It seems odd to read this apparently depressing book on the holiday of happiness. However, King Solomon's brutal confrontation with the transience of life and our temporary accomplishments on earth actually reveals the key to true happiness and security. He concludes, "In the end, obey the word of God and do His bidding, because this is everything."

Sukkot teaches us how to find security and permanence in what seems transient. We embrace the perishable four species and dwell in a makeshift hut covered with biodegradable materials, as we acknowledge that happiness and security are based not on what we possess but on who we are in relationship to God. When we serve God here and now, we infuse the finite world with infinite meaning and connect the fleeting moment to eternity.

When we understand this truth, we will never be in a rush to get to some other place and some future time, because we realize that the joy of life is to serve God and there is no better time than now and no better place then here—so what's the rush? If not now, when?

We often do wrong and sacrifice our integrity in the present because we are anxious to secure our future. Sukkot, however, teaches us that we can find security even in the temporal and transient when we focus our attention on serving God here and now.

Adam and Eve also transgressed because they were impatient. They intuited that eating the fruit of the Tree of

Knowledge of Good and Bad was essential to fulfilling their purpose on earth. And they were right, but their timing was wrong. According to the Kabbalah, God wanted them to eat from the Tree of Knowledge of Good and Bad, but not then. The right time to do it would have been on Shabbat. Had they patiently waited, trusted God, and eaten the fruit as a humble service to Him—rather than as a rebellious act in defiance of Him—they would have accomplished their ultimate goals. They would have actualized their godliness by experiencing God's love and their oneness with God.

Sukkot sets us off on the right foot into the new year by teaching us how to protect ourselves from sadness and evil: trust in God, humble yourself before Him, and only concern yourself with fulfilling His commandments—here and now.

THE CIRCLE OF LOVE

Each morning of Sukkot, near the end of the festive prayer service, we carry our four species, marching in a circle around the cantor (the leader of the service), who holds a *Sefer Torah*, the Torah scroll.

On the last day of Sukkot, which is referred to as Hoshanah Rabah, we encircle the Torah seven times. This number is reminiscent of the seven times the Israelites circled the city of Jericho and the walls came tumbling down. But the day after Hoshanah Rabah—when we celebrate the holiday of Shemini Atzeret, also called Simchat

Torah—we dance in a circle around an empty space hugging the Torah in our arms. Why?

During the seven days of Sukkot, when we circle the Torah, we remind ourselves that Torah must be the center of our lives. If we are self-centered, we cannot love others, nor can we love God. To achieve true love, we need to move ourselves out of the center and put the Torah—which contains the will and wisdom of God—in the center.

Some people, however, claim that the laws of the Torah are actually obstacles to achieving true love. They argue that the rituals, formalities, and minutiae of Torah law interfere with experiencing a warm, personal, individual, spontaneous, and loving relationship with God and other people. They believe that the commandments build walls, not bridges.

This is never true as long as we remember that the laws of the Torah are the will of God and express what God asks of us. True love means doing for your beloved what he or she asks of you—not what you feel like doing even though it is against his or her wishes.

But, even when you understand this basic truth, the commandments could interfere with your loving relationship to God if you perform them mindlessly. The richness of ritual depends on the measure of intention you invest in it. Imagine that you decide to tell your beloved three times a day that you love her. If you don't mean it at all but simply repeat, "I love you," like a parrot, then this mindless routine will become obstructive and destructive to your love.

This is a danger only when we consider the commandments of God to be peripheral to our daily lives. However, when we put the Torah in the center of our lives and acknowledge that it is the axis upon which our lives revolve, then over time the Torah will actually break down the walls that separate us from God. This was the message that God communicated to us through the prophet Isaiah: "It is only your wrongdoings that separate you from Me." The Torah and its commandments, however, break the barriers that divide us and build bonds of love.

After we succeed in making the Torah the center of our lives during Sukkot, and the barriers to love are broken down, then we celebrate the holiday of Simchat Torah by dancing with the Torah around an empty space. Of course, we know that there is no such thing as an empty space, because God's presence fills the earth—there is no place void of God's presence. On Simchat Torah we acknowledge that putting the Torah in the center of our lives empowers us to find the true center, core, and soul of our lives—God.

The celebrations of Sukkot and Simchat Torah prepare us to dance our way into the upcoming year in a circle of love, embracing the natural, holding the hand of our fellow Jew, hugging the Torah, and feeling close to God. And we experience all this in the very midst of our everyday lives in this transient world.

RAIN, RAIN, COME AGAIN

Each day during the Sukkot prayer service, when we march around in a circle, we pray that the New Year be blessed with rain. This is also an appropriate way to celebrate our renewed relationship with God. What makes the prayer for rain so special?

In the Jewish tradition, God is described metaphorically as desiring and even needing our prayers. The book of Genesis describes how, in the process of creation, God had not sent rain that would cause vegetation to grow, because there was no one to work the field. The Midrash explains that there was no human being to recognize the goodness of rain and thus pray for it. In other words, God needed a human being to want rain and ask for it before He could send it pouring down. This story captures the meaning of prayer, the power of humanity, and the nature of our relationship to God.

Even something as fundamental to life as rain, which seems programmed into the nature of the universe, needs our prayers. Why? Because God cannot pour blessings upon us until we want to receive those blessings. For example, our will for health is the receptacle to receive the blessings of well-being. Our will for livelihood is the receptacle to receive the blessings of prosperity.

Prayer is not a passive supplication to God for help. Prayer is a powerful force. Through prayer we make things happen because we want them to happen, and God, so to speak, is waiting to hear what we want. Prayer hooks us up to the motor of our lives: willpower. On Sukkot, as we prepare ourselves for the adventures and challenges of the upcoming year, we need to exercise our basic right to the power of prayer. And we need to realize that if rain needs our prayers, all the more so does everything else in our lives.

On the last day of Sukkot, Hoshanah Rabah, after we complete the seventh circle in our march, we put down the four species and take five separate willow branches. We then recite more prayers for rain and sustenance, and we hit the ground five times with the willows. As mentioned earlier, the willow has no taste or fragrance and therefore represents a person who is unlearned in Torah and does no good deeds. The message of this custom is this: by the end of Sukkot we realize that even if we are unworthy of God's favor, bereft of Torah and good deeds, His love for us is unconditional and He will take care of us. All we have to do is ask.

Now, I bet you are wondering, "What about the beating of the willows against the ground five times? What is that all about?" This was a custom not found in the Torah but instituted by the prophets. Tradition tells us that this custom is filled with much mystical meaning, but these secrets are known only to the greatest of sages. I would suggest that topping off our Sukkot celebration in this mystical manner also teaches us an essential lesson to carry with us into the year. After all the explanations for the meaning behind Judaism, whether you understand the will of God or not—just do it!

BUILDING THE SUKKAH OF FAITH

When we take a bird's-eye view of the holidays that inaugurate the New Year, we see a collection of diverse images of God. The predominant image of God on Rosh Hashanah is as a King and Judge who is writing us into a cosmic

Book of Life and Death. On Yom Kippur we encounter God as a compassionate forgiving Father. Sukkot features God as a Lover, and we feel close to Him and hugged by Him. And on Simchat Torah we reach the height of intimacy and complete union with God. What are we to do with all this imagery? Are we really supposed to believe all this?

Surely all these images are only metaphors for a higher divine truth that is beyond spoken words and conceptual images. We can only know the divine truth experientially. Anyone who believes that God is literally a King, Judge, Father, or Lover is making graven images of God and committing spiritual idolatry.

What then is the meaning and value of all these metaphors?

According to Kabbalah, these conceptual metaphors are vehicles to access the transcendental truth of God. These are the metaphors that can take us to the threshold of the immediate and direct experience of God that is beyond all words and concepts. Any other metaphors wouldn't even get us close to the truth.

Our task and goal on these holy days is to use these metaphors of King, Father, and Lover toward building our consciousness and awareness of God, so that we can receive and experience God's guiding power, forgiveness, and love.

With every word of prayer and every detail of the holiday rituals, we are constructing the necessary channels to bring the divine truth into our lives. Think of these metaphors as the code number to a great combination lock. The Torah gives us the right combination of metaphors necessary to unlock the vault and get to the real treasure of divine truth.

We need to believe that God is like a King and Judge who stands over us and judges us on Rosh Hashanah. We then need to believe that God is also like a forgiving Father, who picks us up, supports us, and forgives us on Yom Kippur. And on Sukkot, we need to believe that God is like our Lover, close to us, holding us in His loving embrace. All these images in combination unlock the door to our intimate communion with God on Simchat Torah.

This is the true meaning and power of faith. Faith is not a collection of ideas that we adopt. It is an orientation to life and to the Source of all life: God. Faith is a way of seeing. Unlike the popular saying "seeing is believing," the Kabbalah teaches, "believing is seeing." In other words, the greater our faith is in God, the more God can become manifest in our lives. The more we believe that God is like a King, the more divine power and guidance can enter our lives. The more we believe that God is like a compassionate Father, the more compassion and forgiveness can become manifest in our lives. And the more we believe that God is like a Lover, the more divine love, intimacy, and oneness can fill our lives. Our major life's work is to build—with proper ideas, words, and actions—a sukkah of faith, a perceptual dwelling that we can take with us even in the desertlike, barren times of our lives.

The more we believe in God's guidance, forgiveness, and love, the more we can receive them.

ANTICIPATION

The mood throughout Sukkot can be best described as the joy of anticipation for the ultimate. Each day of the seven-day festival brings us closer to complete intimacy with God. We finally experience this on Simchat Torah, when we celebrate finishing the yearly cycle of Torah readings and start over again from Genesis. On this great day we dance with the Torah in the most joyous display of affection. While Simchat Torah is the ultimate realization of our connection with God, the sense of anticipation of this union that we feel during Sukkot is even more thrilling than the joy we actually feel on this day.

As counterintuitive as it may seem, in this and other instances, we find that Judaism puts anticipation ahead of realization. The Midrash teaches, for example, that when we finally get to the World to Come, the angels will ask us whether we anticipated the redemption. This is because the anticipation for the redemption itself is considered the greatest joy.

Another example of the weight the Talmudic sages put on the joy of anticipation can be seen in the Simchat Beit HaShoeva ceremony. This ancient ceremony of drawing water from the earth and pouring it on the altar was the highlight of Sukkot celebrations in Temple times. Interestingly, the sages describe the festivities surrounding the *drawing* of the water for the ceremony as the time of ultimate joy, even though this was only the preparation for *pouring* the water on the altar. The anticipation of doing the mitzvah was actually experienced as greater than the fulfillment of the actual mitzvah. The Simchat Beit HaShoeva also expressed the joy of anticipation of the ultimate experience of oneness with God that was achieved on the final day of celebrations—on Simchat Torah, when the celebrants embraced the Torah (which is referred metaphorically as water since its teachings are as fundamental to life as water).

When we think about it, we see this dynamic at work in other aspects of life. Very often people feel that their wedding was not as joyous as their anticipation of the wedding. The best part is the planning and the dreaming, talking about it, choosing the dress, the flowers, and so on. The wedding itself can be a blur. People claim I was at my wedding; there are photographs to prove it, but I really was not there. I remember getting out of the taxi, and then I was gone. I was too overwhelmed to be mentally present.

In our thinking and dreaming and hoping and planning, we feel incredible joy. But afterward, we often find ourselves saying, "It could have been a little more this, a little more that. . . ." This is one of the reasons the water-drawing ceremony, Simchat Beit HaShoeva, was the height of joy, because it stimulated our anticipation of achieving complete intimacy with God on Simchat Torah.

The Talmud teaches that God gave Himself to us in writing. In other words, the Torah embodies the presence of God. When we dance on Simchat Torah hugging the Torah, it is as if we are dancing with and hugging God. And since the Torah is the will and wisdom of God, when we learn the Torah we are completely one with God.

LOVE IS IN THE AIR

To sum it up, the cycle of the High Holidays that begins on Rosh Hashanah and ends on Simchat Torah is all about love.

Available on Rosh Hashanah is a whole new level of awareness of our eternal connection to God, unlike anything we have experienced before. From Rosh Hashanah to Yom Kippur we acknowledge our failings, feel the pain of remorse, and bitterly regret distancing ourselves from God. However, we also realize that the feelings inspired by these days of judgment actually support, empower, and build us.

On Yom Kippur we finally come face-to-face with God and experience His forgiveness. Once the painful load of our wrongdoings and our embarrassment over them is off our shoulders, we begin to feel confident and joyful as we approach and prepare for Sukkot.

On Sukkot God embraces us with love. Though we no longer have a Temple and do not perform the water libation ceremony anymore, we still prepare joyously throughout Sukkot for Simchat Torah—when we celebrate the ultimate intimate connection with God as we dance joyously with the Torah.

On that great day we experience the unparalleled joy of knowing that God is one and we are one with God and each other. We then experience our own godliness, and our true selves radiate with love. And we understand that love was always in the air. We just didn't know it was there.

SEVEN

Chanukah

Celebrating Hope

In the second century B.C.E., the Greek Seleucid emperor Antiochus Epiphanes began a systematic campaign against Judaism, which he saw as an obstacle to the spread of Hellenist philosophy in Israel. He forbade certain forms of religious observance (circumcision, for example); disobedience was punishable by death. He desecrated the Temple by sacrificing pigs there, and he put up a statue of the Greek god Jupiter in the Holy of Holies. Enraged, Mattathias the Maccabee and his five sons recruited a small army of Jews and launched a guerrilla war that is commonly known as the Maccabean revolt.

After three years of aggressive fighting, this small

Jewish army miraculously beat the huge and mighty Greek army. They took back control of Jerusalem and, on the twenty-fifth of the Hebrew month of Kislev, re-dedicated the Temple.

When the Maccabean army came into the Temple to restore it to its original sanctity, they found in the building only one cruse of uncontaminated oil. This small amount could light the candelabra—the menorah—in the Temple for only one day. To press new and ritually fit oil for use in the Temple would take eight days. Nonetheless, they lit the one cruse of oil, fully expecting that it would only last the day. However, the oil miraculously burned for eight days. To celebrate and publicize this miracle annually, Jews light candles for eight days starting on the twenty-fifth of Kislev.

Thus, the holiday of Chanukah ("Dedication") celebrates two miracles: the miraculous military victory and the supernatural phenomenon of one small cruse of oil providing eight days of light. The miracle of the light, however, captures center stage on this holiday, so much so that, according to Jewish law, when we light the candles in celebration of Chanukah, we are prohibited from using their light for any task. We are commanded to simply *look* at the light. All year long we are looking at what we see *in* the light, but on Chanukah we are to focus on seeing the light itself. We are to fill our eyes with the light of Chanukah so that when Chanukah is over, we will continue to see our lives in this special light. What is special about the light of Chanukah?

SEEING THE LIGHT

Most people who know even a little about Kabbalah probably know that it talks a great deal about light—what it calls the Endless Light. It teaches that through our actions we draw and increase this Divine Light into the world or diminish its presence.

For a long time I had difficulty understanding this mystical metaphor until one day it all came together. As a way of explaining this difficult concept, let me ask you to imagine for a moment that you have walked into a magic store that sells special flashlights equipped with different kinds of magic lights. For example, if you shine the "light of science" on your hand, you see not a hand but cells and blood vessels and tendons and ligaments. Another flashlight might be called the "light of art," and if you point it at your hand you see form and color and texture, as if your hand were a painting by Leonardo da Vinci. You are having a lot of fun trying out the different flashlights with the different lights, and then you see one labeled "the light of Chanukah." What will you see in that light?

When King Solomon wrote in his famous work, the book of Ecclesiastes, "Futility of futilities, of what worth is the work of man under the sun," he was talking about what it is like to see the world in the light of the sun, in the light of nature. But the *Zohar* teaches us that when you see the world in the light that comes from *beyond* the sun, then nothing is old, everything is new.

The light of Chanukah is the light beyond the sun; it

is the light beyond nature; it is the light of miracles. And what does the world look like in the light of miracles? The world looks like a miracle. In the light of nature, nothing is new, but in the light of miracles, everything is always miraculously novel. When I point the "light of science" at my hand, I see cells, I see veins. When I point the "light of art" at my hand, I see form, I see shape, and I see color. But when I point the "light of Chanukah" at my hand, I see a miracle.

We fill our eyes with the light of Chanukah for eight days, so that when the holiday is over, we see that everything is a miracle; we see that even nature is really a miracle. And each time we look in this light at our hands, nose, toes, tree, birds, bees, and so on, we are amazed because it is all so new and wondrous. Albert Einstein once said, "There are two ways of looking at the world: either you see nothing as a miracle or you see everything as a miracle." Judaism sees everything as a miracle. Hellenism saw nothing as a miracle. To the Greeks, a miracle was an absurdity. To them, only what was reasonable, logical, and rational could be real. Miracles were illogical and therefore not possible. The Greeks could never access the light of Chanukah, the light of miracles, because they only believed in the light of logic and reason. According to the Greeks, the world always existed; it never was created. History is an inevitable process—the present and the future are linked to the past and are the necessary outcome of the past. Nothing unusual will happen or can happen. History will march on, consequence following consequence. Similarly, their view of God or gods was of superbeings detached from the world. Their gods didn't care about humanity. For the Greeks, nothing was new under the sun. Therefore, miracles were impossible.

This is why Judaism irritated the Greeks so much, and this is why they decided to wipe it out. They first outlawed Shabbat and circumcision and the Jewish protocol for establishing the beginning of a Hebrew month at the onset of a new moon. They focused on those areas because the message of these Jewish rituals contradicted their worldview of reason and logic.

The weekly celebration of Shabbat expresses the Jewish belief that the world is a creation of God and He created it as "something from nothing." Not logical, of course. And why did God create the world? Not because He had to, but because He simply wanted to. The world doesn't exist necessarily; rather, the world is a pure expression of divine will and freedom—a spontaneous act of love. And what's more, when God created the world, He didn't finish it. He left it incomplete so that we could have work to do, so that we could play a role in creation and become God's partners. That's what the book of Genesis means by "God blessed the seventh day and sanctified it, because on it He had abstained from all His work which He created *to do*."

In other words, God created work that needed to be done. God not only created a world, but He created a world that is full of work to do. And we are the ones who are meant to do that work and help complete the world. God wanted a partner to help Him finish the job. Therefore, He created an imperfect, incomplete world in order that He could make a covenant with us to complete it with Him.

To the Greeks, the idea that humanity could be a partner with God was ridiculous. When Greeks would see Jews performing circumcision on their children as a physical sign of this covenant, they thought the act was a horrible mutilation of the perfection of the human body. How can you take nature and in any way imply that you can change it, fix it, or make it better? They reasoned that nature is already perfect, that it's a complete manifestation of reason.

The same goes for the sanctification of the new moon. In accordance with Jewish law, a Jewish court would determine the first day of the upcoming Hebrew month based on the testimony of two witnesses who saw the moon waxing. This tradition demonstrates our belief that we take part in determining time and making history. Again, to the Greeks, this was totally illogical. According to their view, history cannot be changed, and time is a manifestation of reason.

Judaism believes that God created the world, cares about us, and invites us to be His partner in making history and perfecting His creation. The Greeks assumed that the world is perfect already and everything is as it should be. The world is eternal, the events of history are inevitable, and God is impersonal. Therefore, don't expect any favors, don't expect any novelties, don't expect any divine interventions, don't expect miracles, and have no hope. Life is just one big Greek tragedy. Therefore, the Greeks wanted to do away with the Jews and their commitment to Torah life.

Torah study, however, was very interesting to the Greeks. They even had the Torah translated into Greek. But they thought that the Torah was written by human beings and should be studied only for the sake of the human wisdom it contained. To the Greeks, there is no such thing as divinely given wisdom; there is only human wisdom, born out of logic.

However, many things in the Torah simply did not make sense to them.

I find that when people are first exploring Judaism, they often expect it to be logical and explainable. But if we could explain it all, then that would mean that the Torah is completely reasonable and rational. If the Torah were completely reasonable and rational, we wouldn't need a God to reveal it. A human being could reveal such a Torah. But if the Torah is a prophetic divine revelation, then there are obviously going to be laws and commandments in it that are beyond our rationale. It is essential to understand that the purpose of the Torah and its commandments is not simply to teach wisdom and offer good advice for better living. The Torah and the commandments express the will of God—what God wants us to do. They enable us to establish a personal loving relationship with God.

If the only things I was willing to do for my wife were the things that make sense to me, we might have a lot of arguments. But shouldn't I do what my loved one asks of me just because I love her? To fulfill her request is an opportunity to show her love and bond with her.

This is also true of our relationship to God, our Ultimate Loved One.

Of course, the Greeks did not believe that people should be trying to bond with deities. To them, a deity was an object for meditation. What's love got to do with it? For the Greeks, intelligence was the highest achievement of the human being. And if the Jews studied Torah for that purpose, well, then, fine. But for the Jews, the highest achievements of the human being were and continue to be responsibility and moral excellence. We value intelligence, we value learning, but that is because we believe that learning—God's law, the Torah—nurtures our loving relationship with God and leads us to be more moral. God loves us and cares for us, and therefore He gave us His Torah so that we can bond with Him and experience His love for us.

THE MYSTERY OF HISTORY

When we live life in the light of miracles, in the light of hope, in the light of Judaism, we see that the present is not a mere consequence of the past. The present can be defined not only by the past but also by the future.

Yes, the future.

That's why there could be a miracle. A miracle happens when God, for the sake of His future plan for humanity, interferes with the natural transition from past into present—just because the world has to get to a certain place.

That is a quirk in the Jewish perspective of history. Unlike the world's perspective of history, which sees events unfolding out of the past, as if the past were pushing history forward, the Jewish perspective sees the future activating history, so that history is actually being pulled, not pushed, toward the future.

If sometimes—because we have free will as God's partner in making history—history goes off the track, then God might interfere. Then the present may not be determined by the past—it may be determined by the future. That's when miracles happen.

One key example of that is the survival of the Jewish people, which historians and philosophers have puzzled over for centuries. As Mark Twain (who was not Jewish) wrote in his famous essay "Concerning the Jews," published in *Harper's* magazine in 1897:

> If the statistics are right, the Jews constitute but one percent of the human race. It suggests a nebulous dim puff of star dust lost in the blaze of the Milky Way. Properly the Jew ought hardly to be heard of; but he is heard of, has always been heard of. He is as prominent on the planet as any other people, and his importance is extravagantly out of proportion to the smallness of his bulk.
>
> His contributions to the world's list of great names in literature, science, art, music, finance,

medicine, and abstruse learning are also way out of proportion to the weakness of his numbers. He has made a marvelous fight in this world, in all the ages; and he has done it with his hands tied behind him. He could be vain of himself, and be excused for it.

The Egyptian, the Babylonian, and the Persian rose, filled the planet with sound and splendor, then faded to dream-stuff and passed away; the Greek and the Roman followed, and made a vast noise, and they are gone; other peoples have sprung up and held their torch high for a time, but it burned out, and they sit in twilight now, or have vanished.

The Jew saw them all, beat them all, and is now what he always was, exhibiting no decadence, no infirmities of age, no weakening of his parts, no slowing of his energies, no dulling of his alert and aggressive mind. All things are mortal, but the Jew; all other forces pass, but he remains. What is the secret of his immortality?

The great French philosopher Blaise Pascal came to the same conclusion. In his book *Pensees* he writes:

It is certain that in certain parts of the world we can see a peculiar people, separated from the other peoples of the world and this is called the Jewish people. . . . This people is not only of remarkable antiquity but has also lasted for a singular long time. . . . For whereas the people of Greece and Italy, of Sparta, Athens and Rome, and others who came so much later, have perished so long ago, these still exist, despite the efforts of so many powerful kings who have tried a hundred times to wipe them out, as historians testify, and as can easily be judged by the natural order of things over such a long spell of years. They have always been preserved, however, and their preservation was foretold. . . .

We should not be here. We broke all the historical rules. No other nation has survived under these kinds of conditions. We are a people of miracles who believe in a God of miracles. We believe in a God who cares, a God who loves us. And if God so wills it, something radical and new can happen at any moment. We have reason to be unreasonable and, therefore, to be hopeful.

This is why we light candles on Chanukah and bring the light of Chanukah—the light of miracles—into our lives every year. We fill our eyes with that light so that we can use it all year long, once we've internalized it within ourselves. In fact, it is only in the light of Chanukah that we can understand Chanukah at all. It's only because the Maccabees had the light of miracles already in their souls that they managed to accomplish something very unreasonable and very irrational. A small group of inexperienced fighters stood up against the mighty warriors of the Greek Empire and won. But they never doubted it. They knew that victory was possible, because God created the world and is free to do as He pleases.

FREE LOVE

The Maccabean victory was a miracle in itself, so why did God top it off by keeping the menorah miraculously lit for eight days? When you think of it, this miracle was not only very strange but unnecessary. If the Maccabees had been able to light the menorah for only one day, the Jewish people would not have crumbled. Yes, they would have had to wait another eight days, but would that have been so terrible?

But that is the very definition of miracle: it's unnecessary. Natural phenomena are necessary. If I put a drop of ink into water, it will necessarily dissolve. That's nature. But a miracle is just the opposite. It doesn't have to be—indeed, in the light of nature, it *shouldn't* be. But it is, because God wants it to be. God needs no reason to make a miracle. God wants to, and God does it. That's why Chanukah is such an incredible holiday, because it really celebrates the essence of miracles, the essence of the unnecessary.

When you look at the world in the light of Chanukah, you realize that the world is completely unnecessary, that you're unnecessary, that everything is unnecessary. And yet the world is here, and you are here.

Celebrating the unnecessary is really the celebration of love. Because the ultimate expression of love and kindness is not in doing what I have to do but in doing what I don't have to do. If I drive over your rosebush, crushing it under the wheels of my SUV, and then offer to replace it, that is not an act of love—it is the law and I have to do it. But if one day, just because I want to and not because I have to, I buy you a dozen roses, that is an act of love. If I buy my son a sweater for his fifth birthday, that's nice, but he will not see it as a great sign of my love because he needs a sweater. But if I buy him a toy—which he could live without—then to him my love is free and over-flowing.

Judaism believes that we are here by the grace of God, because God, out of His infinite love, freely created us. He did not need to create us. He simply wanted to. It is a miracle that we are here, and on Chanukah, more than any other time of the year, we see that, and we marvel. We see ourselves in the light of miracles, in the light of love and hope.

And just as God's love is manifest in doing the unnecessary for us, we too act in kind to show our love for God and light more candles than necessary. According to Jewish law, each household is obligated to light only one candle each day of the eight days of Chanukah. However, we go beyond what is required, and each member of the household lights an individual menorah, and each day we add a light. Therefore, on the first day of Chanukah we light one light, but on the second day we light two, on the third day three, until we reach the eighth day and light eight lights.

Without the light of Chanukah we would be totally

blind to the true Chanukah victory—the triumph of God's love for us and our love for God. It is only in the light of Chanukah that we are able to see the infinite and miraculous possibilities of love. In the light of science and in the light of art we see aspects—and only *some* aspects—of what is. But in the light of Chanukah, in the light of miracles, we see all that is and all that can be.

In the light of Chanukah we see that everything is a miracle, that anything is possible, and that hope shines eternal.

—EIGHT—

Tu B'Shvat

Celebrating Pleasure

Tu B'Shvat is not mentioned in the Bible. The oldest reference is found in the Talmud, where Tu B'Shvat is called "the new year of the trees," and, strangely, it is not described as any kind of holiday to be celebrated. The Talmud ascribes significance to this date only in terms of the legal implications of taking tithes (10 percent) from fruits. According to Jewish law, one is not allowed to take tithes for the priests and the poor from a previous year's produce to substitute for this year's. We learn that Tu B'Shvat—the fifteenth of the month of Shvat on the Hebrew calendar—is the date that distinguishes last year's produce from this year's.

More recently, that is, about five hundred years ago,

the Kabbalists of Tsfat revealed a deeper understanding of Tu B'Shvat, transforming it into the holiday we celebrate today. They taught that Tu B'Shvat is an opportune time for fixing the transgression of Adam and Eve. Amazingly, just through the simple act of eating fruit during the Tu B'Shvat festive dinner, we are able to contribute to this cosmic repair.

But how? How are we fixing the transgression of Adam and Eve, according to the Kabbalists?

First, let's explore the transgression of Adam and Eve, and then we can understand why the Kabbalists created the holiday of Tu B'Shvat and why eating fruit is the way we celebrate it.

The Torah says that God put Adam and Eve in the garden "to work it and to guard it." The Jewish oral tradition teaches us that this refers to the dos and don'ts of the Torah. The dos are called the positive mitzvot, and the don'ts are called the negative mitzvot. Adam and Eve were given a very small thing to do: eat from all the trees of the garden. And their single prohibition was not to eat fruit from the Tree of Knowledge of Good and Bad. What was that about?

The Torah teaches that God created the world so that we could experience goodness in general and His goodness in particular. Experiencing His goodness—bonding with God—is the greatest joy imaginable. God empowers us to bond with Him by serving His purpose for creation. Just as when we do for others we feel connected to them, so too serving God enables us to bond with Him. Ironically, serving God is actually self-serving—profoundly fulfilling and pleasurable.

If we eat and enjoy the fruits of this world for God's sake—because this is what He asks of us—then we are actually serving God and bonding with Him. We serve God by acknowledging that the fruits of this world are His gifts to us and by willingly accepting and enjoying those gifts. The root of Jewish life is, in fact, enjoyment—the pleasure of connecting to God. We connect to God by serving Him, and this means obeying His command to enjoy the fruits of this world.

While in the Garden of Eden, Adam and Eve's entire obligation was to enjoy all the lush fruits—with the notable exception of one forbidden fruit. Sure enough, they went after that one. This misdeed demonstrated their confused orientation to the real meaning of pleasure. Rather than seeing the fruits as pleasurable because they are God's gifts and enjoying them as part of their service to God, they wanted to partake of them independently of God—in fact, contrary to His will.

THE ART OF RECEIVING

As already explained, real pleasure is experiencing a connection with God. We enjoy the ultimate spiritual pleasure when we enjoy the physical pleasures of this world as part of our divine service. Then the act of receiving and enjoying God's gifts to us is amazingly transformed into a selfless act of serving God.

We can understand now that God's only desire in giving Adam and Eve those two mitzvot was to give them the ultimate pleasure—bonding with Him. True pleasure was not in the taste of the fruits but in eating and enjoying these gifts from God. This was the way to serve and connect with Him—the ultimate pleasure.

But Adam and Eve misunderstood this. They did not see physical pleasure as a conduit to the spiritual pleasure of bonding with God. Rather, they sought pleasure independent of God. This is the root of all wrongdoing. Do we see the pleasures of this world as a gift from God, enjoying them in the service of God and using them as conduits to a connection to God? Or do we seek pleasure independent of any connection to God? In other words, is the pleasure about us, or is the pleasure about our relationship with God?

There is a fundamental difference between *having* pleasure and *receiving* pleasure. If we want to have pleasure, it doesn't matter where it comes from. Having pleasure is void of any connection to a reality greater than ourselves. It is simply a selfish desire to experience a particular pleasure for its own sake. Receiving pleasure, however, is rooted in the soul's desire to serve God's purpose, which is to receive the ultimate joy of connecting to Him.

Adam and Eve ate the forbidden fruit because they were totally confused about their purpose on earth and, consequently, what is truly pleasurable in this world. They were clueless about what would bring them meaning and joy in life.

Following Adam and Eve's fatal mistake, God told them, "Because you ate from the tree that I commanded you not to eat from, the earth has become cursed." God was not punishing the earth because of Adam and Eve's transgression; rather, He was informing them that their distorted orientation toward physical pleasures had turned the earth into a curse rather than a blessing for them and their descendants.

Depending on how we view the physical world, it is cursed or blessed. If we look at the physical world as a conduit to a connection with God and if, as a service to God, we gratefully receive His gift of delicious fruits, we thereby experience His presence and the physical world becomes blessed. The physical world then becomes a bridge between the human and the divine. But if we become fixated on the physical, independent of any relationship with God, and mistakenly perceive this world as the source of our pleasure rather than as a bridge to God, then this world becomes a barrier to God and a curse for us.

Now that we understand the transgression of Adam and Eve, we can begin to appreciate how we can contribute to fixing it on Tu B'Shvat. On Tu B'Shvat the new sap begins to rise up into the trees. And we bring abundance to this process when we celebrate Tu B'Shvat.

The Talmud says that more than a baby wants to suck, a mother wants to nurse. The mother not only gets tremendous pleasure from nursing her baby, but the flow of her milk is actually generated by its sucking. The more the baby wants to suck, the more milk the mother has to give. This principle also applies to our relationship to God.

As mentioned earlier, God wants to give us the greatest of all pleasures, which is a connection with Him. But if we don't recognize that to be the greatest pleasure and we don't want it, then He can't give it to us. Of course God could give it to us, but it would just be a waste, because we wouldn't recognize it for what it is.

I find this to be a frightening idea—there's something God can't do. He can't force us to want what He has to give us. He wants to give us the best, the ultimate, but we are distracted. We want material possessions, because we are confused about what is really worth wanting. We may even be oblivious of what constitutes true pleasure and the greatest joy possible.

God wants to give us the greatest gift—Himself; a connection to the ultimate—and we are looking for transitory pleasures that are here today and gone tomorrow. One Jewish philosopher described our confused lives as a "graveyard of pleasures," because as soon as we get what we so long to have, it's gone. The greatest failure in our pursuit of transient pleasures is achieving them, because as soon as we eat that gourmet dinner, it's gone. The opposite is true in the ecstatic pleasure of connecting to God. As soon as we experience God, we're able to continue to expand that experience and enjoy an even greater experience of God. The spiritual adventure is endless.

The Torah says that the generation of the Flood saddened God with its evil deeds. Although the Torah is filled with anthropomorphic descriptions of God, it seems a little much to describe God as sad. But Rabbi Obadiah

Sforno, the sixteenth-century Italian biblical commentator, explains that God is sad when we are not receptive to the gift He wants to give us—His presence in our lives. This causes God great sadness, similar to a nursing woman whose baby does not want to suck and refuses to be breastfed.

THE POWER OF A BLESSING

On Tu B'Shvat we attempt to fix the transgression of Adam and Eve when we enjoy the fruits of the earth preceded by the recitation of an appreciative blessing to God: "Blessed are you, God . . ."; in other words, "God, You are the source of this blessing."

An apple is not just an apple; an apple is a blessing. Maybe I could believe that apples come from trees but a blessing could only come from God. If I really contemplate the mystery and miracle of the taste, fragrance, beauty, and nutrition wrapped up in this apple, I see that it's more than just a fruit—it is a wondrous loving gift from God. When I taste an apple with that kind of consciousness, I cannot but experience the presence of God within the physical. When I recite a blessing before I eat and acknowledge food as a gift from God, I reveal the divinity within it and the transient sensual pleasure of the food is transformed, because it is filled with eternal spiritual pleasure. The food then feeds not only my body but also my soul. However, when I eat without a blessing, it's as if I stole the food. Perhaps it will nourish and bring pleasure to my body, but it will do nothing for my soul.

The soul is nourished only when it experiences its eternal connection to God.

Tu B'Shvat is an opportune time to celebrate how eating and enjoying the fruits of trees can be a bridge to God and how it can bring back the blessing to the earth. When we enjoy the fruits of the previous year as wonderful gifts from God and affirm our yearning for God's presence manifest in the fruit, we are like a baby sucking its mother's milk with great appetite. We draw forth with great abundance the "milk of the earth"—the sap rises up with great abundance, so that the trees will bear much fruit in the coming year.

Unlike Adam and Eve, who sought pleasure separate from God and who turned physical pleasure into a barrier to God, on Tu B'Shvat we enjoy the fruits as God's gift and experience their pleasure as a connection to God. In this way we fix the transgression of Adam and Eve. We free the earth from being a curse for us—a barrier to God. We transform it into a bridge so that it becomes a wellspring of blessing and God-given pleasure.

On Tu B'Shvat we put a special emphasis on eating the seven types of fruits that represent the unique agricultural benefits of the Holy Land of Israel. In this way we reinforce our extraordinary connection to the land promised to us by God. Historically, it's known that when the Jews were exiled from the land of Israel, the land ceased to produce—it lay barren even though it was known as the Fertile Crescent.

A non-Jewish witness (Mark Twain again) described it

in this way at the end of the nineteenth century in *Innocents Abroad*:

> We traversed some miles of desolate country whose soil is rich enough but is given wholly to weeds—a silent, mournful expanse. . . . A desolation is here that not even imagination can grace with the pomp of life and action. We reached Tabor safely. . . . We never saw a human being on the whole route. We pressed on toward the goal of our crusade, renowned Jerusalem. The further we went the hotter the sun got and the more rocky and bare, repulsive and dreary the landscape became. . . . There was hardly a tree or a shrub anywhere. Even the olive and the cactus, those fast friends of a worthless soil, had almost deserted the country. No landscape exists that is more tiresome to the eye than that which bounds the approaches to Jerusalem. . . . Jerusalem is mournful, dreary and lifeless. I would not desire to live here. It is a hopeless, dreary, heartbroken land.

However, when the Jews returned home, the land came back to life and blossomed. Even the desert now blooms with lush produce.

The Talmud teaches that the surest sign that the Jewish people's redemption has begun is when the land of Israel bears its fruit again. To see the redemption in our time, all you need to do is visit Jerusalem's farmer's market, Machane Yehuda. There you will see the incredibly lush, rich, and delicious fruits of the land of Israel being sold at unbelievable low prices, simply because they are so plentiful here. But a hundred years ago this land was barren!

Why is it that, without the Jews, the land did not bear its fruits?

The people who lived here wanted this land, as any people want any land—for their physical pleasure and material wealth. But for this very reason, the land of Israel did not yield its bounty to them because, as already explained, the physical becomes blessed only to the extent that it's a bridge to God. As soon as the physical becomes a barrier to God, it becomes a curse.

On Tu B'Shvat Jews reinforce their right to the land of Israel by planting trees and enjoying the fruits of the land, thanking God for giving us this land, as explicitly stated numerous times in the Torah. In this way, we express our desire for God's gift and God is, so to speak, able to give it to us even more.

What's really challenging the Jewish people today is not the claims of the Palestinians. It's us. Do *we* want the land of Israel? And do we want it for the right reason?

The right reason to want it is that it's a gift from God, and as such a vehicle to receive the presence of God into our lives. As soon as we lose consciousness of this truth, we will lose parts of our land. This is not because God doesn't want to give it to us—He simply can't give us something we don't want.

God orchestrates the events in our lives and in history in order to wake us up, so that we will be moved to want what He wants to give us. In the meantime we waste much time wanting what we can't have or not wanting what we do have, and not wanting what God waits to give us.

PHYSICAL VERSUS SPIRITUAL

The celebration of Tu B'Shvat captures one of the most fundamental principles of Judaism and how it differs from some other religions. Judaism does not see the physical as inherently cursed. There are other traditions that see the physical world as a distraction, a curse, and the root of evil. Therefore, they teach that the holier you want to be, the more removed you need to be from the material world and its physical pleasures. The holy person does not get married; the holy person lives a celibate life. But this is not the Torah's way to God.

The Star of David hints at Judaism's vision of integration. The two inverted triangles merged into each other represent the harmony of heaven and earth—the union of opposites. The triangle with its base at the top suggests the great divine abundance pouring into us. The triangle with its base at the bottom suggests the vast physical world as it reaches up toward God, making of itself a vessel to receive His bounty. As a symbol of Judaism, the Star of David depicts a religion of connection and integration, not of fragmentation and separation. The goal of Judaism is to be whole—body and soul together, the spiritual and physical united. God is one and His presence fills and unites all, as we read in the book of Jeremiah: "I, God, fill heaven and earth." Not just heaven but also earth.

Our challenge is not in revealing the presence of God in the spiritual heavenly realms. That's easy. Rather, our task is to reveal God's presence on earth. We are not living on planet Earth in order to fix the spiritual. The spiritual is already perfect. Our challenge is to fix the physical realm and show how the divine completely permeates the physical realm, how the physical and spiritual are one although not one and the same.

THE TU B'SHVAT FEAST

At the Tu B'Shvat feast, we consume thirty different kinds of fruits. Upon eating each type, we recite a corresponding verse from the Torah. These thirty fruits comprise three groups of ten, each group representing a different category of fruits: those with inedible shells, such as oranges; those with inedible pits, such as dates; and those that are completely edible, such as figs. These three categories correlate to the three spiritual dimensions of existence, according to the Kabbalah. The type of fruit that has an inedible shell around it is associated with the world of action. This is our world, and it operates from the perception of fragmentation in the universe. The type of fruit that has a hidden, inedible pit—and therefore can't be completely enjoyed—corresponds to the world of formation. This world comes closer to expressing the oneness of God that permeates all; however, it is not completely revealed. Finally, the type of fruit that is completely edible represents the perspective of the world of creation. This is the world that is encompassed by and filled with the presence of God.

The Tu B'Shvat feast celebrates these three categories of fruit, acknowledging the various levels of perceiving and enjoying God's presence. We also drink different types of wine—white, blush, rosé, and red—which hint at the four seasons.

The message of the feast, and the message of Tu B'Shvat, is that the more we enjoy the physical world as a gift from God, the more it becomes a bridge to God. The more we experience the presence of God within the physical, the more we affirm that God's oneness encompasses and permeates everything.

NINE

Purim

Celebrating Trust

Purim celebrates God's rescue of the Jews from an annihilation plot cooked up by the prime minister of the Persian Empire, the evil Haman, in the fourth century B.C.E. Some of the observances of the holiday—such as hearing the Purim story read from the book of Esther and enjoying a festive meal—are obvious ways to celebrate the deliverance. But the other customs of the day have no apparent connection to what happened on Purim.

Why are we required to give charity to the poor, send two food items to a friend, and get so drunk that we do not know the difference between Haman, the villain, and Mordechai, the hero of the story? (This last custom,

I understand, is rigorously kept in college dorms all year round.) What is behind the custom to dress up in costumes? And why do we eat marmalade-stuffed pastries called in Yiddish hamantaschen ("Haman's hats") and in Hebrew *Oznei Haman* ("Haman's ears")? Imagine that you didn't know much about Jewish culinary customs and you walked into a bakery before Purim, only to hear a Hasidic guy in front of you order "a dozen Haman's ears." Over the counter they hand him something with black stuff in the middle, which he gives to his little children. And the kids munch away happily, saying, "I love these Haman's ears." Doesn't that sound sick? Why would anyone want to eat a body part of a sadistic anti-Semite?

There is another bizarre bit about Purim. According to the Jewish oral tradition, this holiday—unlike the other holidays—will be celebrated even after the final redemption at the end of days. The Purim story and the message it conveys will not pale in the light of the ultimate truth revealed in the messianic age and the awesome events that will happen then. While the reading of the other scriptural writings, such as the book of Ruth, Lamentations, and others, will be nullified in the future, the book of Esther will be the only book remaining alongside the Five Books of Moses (the Torah). This is very strange. What could be so important about the book of Esther that it equals the importance and value of the Torah? Purim is a terrific holiday, but why does it hold such great significance for the Jewish people that it seemingly outshines (and will outlast) the other holidays?

BEYOND EITHER-OR

In Hebrew the book of Esther is called *Megillat Ester*. *Megillah*, meaning "scroll," is related to *gilui*, "revelation," while *Ester* is related to *hester*, "hiddenness." So, *Megillat Ester* suggests "the revelation of hiddenness."

The hiddenness revealed on Purim is the hidden omnipresent oneness of God. On Purim we celebrate the true meaning of God's absolute oneness. And since the meaning and truth of God's absolute oneness—the ultimate message of Judaism—is so completely revealed on Purim, this holiday and its story will be relevant and celebrated even in the messianic age.

Understanding the profound meaning of God's oneness requires thinking beyond either-or, but that is not what we are used to.

Once, in a library in Toronto, I came across a reference book that outlined the position of every major philosopher on every major philosophical issue. It was arranged in such a way that I didn't have to read all their writings to get the final conclusions. For example, in the chapter called "Body versus Soul" were listed the arguments of the philosophers who say that human beings are only body/matter and the arguments of the philosophers who say that human beings are essentially spiritual. In the chapter called "Choice versus Determinism" were listed the arguments of those who say, "History is predetermined; man has no free choice" and of those who say, "Man has absolute free choice."

I thought to myself, "This is such a funny book." Judaism's answers, which were not included in any list, are beyond both sides of the argument—neither body nor soul, neither fate nor choice. Judaism's answers are beyond either-or.

To the question "Well, are we a body or a soul?" Judaism would say yes.

"Free choice or fate?" Again, Judaism would say yes.

But can our dualistic minds grasp this paradigm of "beyond either-or"? Yes, after a few good drinks on Purim.

On Purim we are commanded to get so drunk we can't tell the difference between blessed be Mordechai (the leader of the Jews) and cursed be Haman (the evil man who wanted to commit genocide). Some explain that these two Hebrew phrases—"blessed Mordechai" and "cursed Haman"—have the same numerical value: 502 (Hebrew letters also correlate with numbers). But how could "cursed Haman" be equal to the "blessed Mordechai"?

It is plainly true that good and evil are opposites, certainly not of equal value. But the oneness of God that is exalted on Purim transcends the either-or and includes opposites within it.

As we discussed in chapter 5, God is not just the one and only ruling power and there are no other gods; God is absolutely the one and only reality: there is nothing but God and we exist within God. We are souls—sparks, aspects, and expressions of God—and we do not exist apart from Him but rather within Him. Our realization of this truth is an evolving process whereby we discover how united we are with God and each other. This realization of oneness is the ultimate experience of love.

Therefore, when Judaism asserts that God is one, it does not mean "one" in the dictionary sense of "the opposite of many." The oneness of God is the power of love, which transcends and includes both one and many. It includes opposites in a simple oneness. Although our logical minds cannot understand this paradoxical oneness, we get a taste of it on Purim, because the story of Purim aptly illustrates that even the evil person who denies God and rebels against His will serves to reveal God's truth and brings blessing to the world—and in so doing is equal to the good.

The oneness of God is such that He can create us with free choice, and we can choose to go against His will, and yet, mysteriously, we cannot oppose His will. Even though we have free choice, any choice we make still remains within the context of God's being and the confines of God's will. We are free to disobey and do other than God's will, but, because we exist within God, we are not able to undermine His plan.

This is how this ironic truth is revealed in *Megillat Ester*: The story begins with the king's party, in celebration of the seventieth anniversary of the destruction of the Temple in Jerusalem. The prominent Jews of Persia are invited and attend, drinking and carousing at an event where the sacred vessels stolen from the Temple are being used. Fully aware of this conflict of interest, the Jews find it more important to rub elbows with Persia's royalty than to stand loyal to their holy tradition—a typical sign of Jewish assimilation throughout history. But, as has also happened throughout Jewish history, the more the Jews try to assimilate, the more hated they become.

As the story continues, we learn that Haman, the king's prime minister, decides to destroy the Jewish people and proceeds to execute his plot. The irony of the story is that everything he does to destroy the Jews ends up destroying him. For example, Haman builds a gallows on which to hang Mordechai, and that is the very gallows on which he himself is hanged. Moreover, by threatening the Jews' existence, Haman indirectly initiates a renewal of their commitment to Torah, thus reversing the tide of assimilation—always the greatest threat to Jewish survival. Now we can understand why the sweet treat of the holiday is called "Haman's ears." That bitter, destructive man turned out to be the source of sweetness and nourishment for Jewish survival.

Haman's greatest punishment was realizing that his action helped to save the Jewish people. The Talmud teaches that God is equally praised in *gehinnom* (hell) by the evil ones there as He is by the holy ones in *gan eden* (paradise). In other words, the evil ones also end up serving God's plan and revealing His oneness, albeit against their own will and amid a great deal of self-inflicted suffering.

THE NATURAL MIRACLE OF PURIM

In the Purim story, there are no miraculous divine interventions such as we saw in the Passover story. There are no supernatural plagues and no splitting of any seas. In fact, God's name is not even mentioned once in the entire *Megillat Ester*. But the miracle of Purim is actually greater than the miracle of Passover because the ultimate revelation of God's oneness happens when He does not have to openly interfere. This is the meaning of the *Megillat Ester*—the revelation of hiddenness. Hidden within the natural world, within the free choice of people, God's plan is being completely fulfilled, step by step.

When God is depicted in the battle against evil, this is not the ultimate manifestation of His absolute oneness and almighty ruling power. The greatest manifestation of God's truth is when we understand that God does not have to fight the villain. No matter what choices the villain makes, he completely plays into and fulfills God's plan.

This is why, according to the Jewish oral tradition, as soon as the Hebrew month of Adar begins, we should be happy and engage in activities that increase our joy. Although Purim is celebrated only on the fourteenth of the month of Adar, and in some places on the fifteenth, the whole month is identified with happiness. Purim is so abundant with joy that its celebration overflows into the entire month, from beginning to end.

Biblical commentators long ago questioned why this is not so with the month of Nissan, in which the outright miracles of Passover occurred. After all, it was in Nissan that God performed supernatural feats to save the Jews from Egyptian slavery. On Passover we celebrate the miracles of the ten plagues, the supernaturally speedy exit of the Jews from Egypt, and the splitting of the sea.

Although Passover makes us happy, it also makes us a little sad, because it is not the greatest revelation of God's oneness and love. While the open miracles of Passover affirm God's love and power to intervene on behalf of His beloved children, pass over judgment, overrule the laws of nature, and overcome natural limitations and obstacles, they also involve force and violation. The Hebrew word for miracle is *nes*, which is associated with the Hebrew word *ones*, meaning "to coerce." When God performs an outright miracle, He forces and violates nature in order to act against it.

But the events of Purim are a higher revelation of God's truth, illustrating how God works through humanity and within nature. Within nature we see harmony and cooperation. Rather than crushing all the forces that are against us, God uses them toward our future good. Because God is one, there is no confrontation between God and humanity, between the divine and the natural. Nature and humanity are not violated by God's oneness but included within it and filled with it.

The hidden miracles of Purim reveal that His ruling power works through the choices of humanity and that His love for us is hidden within every occurrence and challenge of our lives. Therefore, we can trust that God's love and care is concealed even in the worst times of our lives. On Purim we acknowledge that God's love for us is not only unconditional but also ever-present and eternal. On Purim we celebrate trust in God.

IT'S YOUR CHOICE

One of the greatest feelings of joy is to know and experience life in holy harmony with God. Because of God's all-pervasive oneness and love, we can never really go off course. We are always on target. Our task, however, is to know and feel this in our daily lives.

God has written a script, and we are the actors in that drama. The question is not whether we are going to play our parts, but *how* we will play our parts—consciously and willingly or resisting all the way. We can choose to work for God's plan of growth, love, and oneness, or we can choose to work against it. But God's will *will* be done on earth as it is in heaven—always.

This truth is dramatically illustrated in *Megillat Ester*. Esther—who, unbeknownst to all, is Jewish—has by a strange set of circumstances been forced to marry the king of Persia. (Sounds like fate at work?) But soon after, Haman the prime minister begins to execute his plot to destroy the Jewish people. Upon learning of his plan, Mordechai, who is Esther's uncle, says to her, "Perhaps God has orchestrated things in this very manner so that you could be queen and in a position to save the Jewish people."

But Esther is not convinced. She tells Mordechai, "You know the rules of the palace. If I go to the king without being invited, he could have me killed!"

To that Mordechai says something very bizarre: "If you don't do this, Esther, the salvation of the Jews will come from someplace else."

What kind of argument is that? I mean, if you want to get somebody to do something, what method do you use? Guilt! Mordechai should have said to Esther, "If you don't do it, the Jewish people will be destroyed. This will be the end of Jewish history."

Instead he says, "If you don't do it, the Jews will be saved anyway, but you'll lose out on the starring role."

Mordechai was teaching Esther the great secret of choice: In terms of God's great plan, it does not make a difference what you do. But in terms of your own life, it makes all the difference in the world. Do you want to actively, consciously participate in God's plan or not? If you do not sign on, it will still happen. But you will lose out. You can be the star or an extra on the set. It is your choice.

We have a similar choice in our own generation. We can choose the role we want to play in history right now. Do we want a bit part, or do we want to be one of the leads? Esther decided to take the lead in her time. Risking her life by approaching the king without permission, she revealed that she was Jewish and that someone was plotting to murder her along with her people. The king was aghast but, surprisingly, not one bit disturbed by the news of her heritage. He had Haman hung (on the very gallows that were prepared for Mordechai) and appointed Mordechai the prime minister in Haman's stead. The Jewish people were saved and *Megillat Ester* was written with Esther in the starring role, because she chose to play her part.

On Purim we celebrate that everything in the world

goes according to God's plan—whether we see it or not. On Purim we read the *Megillat Ester* and celebrate the revelation of God's hiddenness within the choices of humanity. To emulate God, the Master of Disguise, we too dress up in disguises. God's plan disguises itself and plays out even through the evil people of the world. But on Purim we actually see that it is a disguise. There is only one actor, playing a myriad of roles. God is absolutely one and only.

THE ONENESS OF THE JEWISH PEOPLE

To mirror God's oneness, the all-inclusive power of love, we do things on Purim that express love and reinforce the oneness of the Jewish people, such as exchanging gifts of food and giving to the poor.

When Haman approached the king to destroy the Jewish people, he inadvertently revealed the secret of the Jewish people. He said, "You know, King, there is one people who are scattered and spread out among the whole empire, and we can destroy them." He mistakenly thought that because we were scattered and diversified, we could be annihilated. However, he unconsciously expressed precisely why he could not succeed, the very reason for the miraculous survival of the Jewish people. We may be scattered and diversified, yet we are still one people. The oneness of the Jewish people reflects the transcendental oneness of God—the essence of love. God's oneness can include multiplicity and diversity, while mysteriously remaining one, and so too can the oneness of the Jewish people.

The Jewish people are very diverse. We are all very different. We all have strong opinions; as the joke goes, "Two Jews, three opinions." And yet we are one.

Because this is a chapter on Purim, jokes are appropriate. So here is another:

A rabbi gets a new position in a synagogue. It is his first day on the job, and the congregation gets to the point in the prayer service where they recite the Shema, "Hear O Israel, the Lord is our God, the Lord is one." At that moment, half of the congregation stands up, while the other half stays seated. Those standing start screaming at the ones sitting down, "Stand up, stand up, it's the Shema!" The ones sitting down say, "Oh, you're crazy! Sit down, sit down, it's the Shema!" The rabbi had never seen anything like this.

The next day the same thing happens. The ones who stand up start yelling at the ones sitting down, and the ones sitting down start yelling at the ones standing up. After a week of this, the rabbi can't take it any longer. He decides to seek out one of the founding members of the synagogue to find out what the original tradition was and settle the argument once and for all. He finds one— Mr. Schwartz, now ensconced in an old folks' home— and goes to visit him along with a member of each of the opposing camps.

The delegate of those who sit asks, "Mr. Schwartz, is it not true that the tradition of the synagogue always was that we sit when we recite the Shema?"

Mr. Schwartz says, "No, that's not the way it was."

"Aha!" cries the delegate of those who stand, "the tradition always was that we stand when we say the Shema!"

Mr. Schwartz shakes his head, "No, that's not the way it was."

So the rabbi says, "Mr. Schwartz, I'm a new rabbi here. Please, you must help me figure this out. Every single day the ones who stand up yell at the ones sitting down, and the ones sitting down yell at the ones standing up."

Mr. Schwartz, with a smile, replies, "That's the way it was!"

That is the Jewish people in a nutshell. What other nation in the world has a book of disputes—called the Talmud—that it considers holy? How can there be holiness in disputes? How can people have opposite opinions and still remain part of one people?

The oneness of the Jewish people is not sameness. Our oneness reflects God's oneness, which includes multiplicity and even encompasses opposites. On Purim we celebrate God's oneness and we celebrate our oneness, by showing love to each other with gifts of food and charity to the poor.

THE PARADOX OF PURIM

We can now appreciate another interesting detail about Purim—it occurs in the month of Adar, whose symbol is Pisces: two fish going in opposite directions.

Pisces is a paradox—it represents oneness that can include opposites. According to astrology, people who are born in the month of Pisces are masters of disguise. They can include within themselves the diversity of all the personality types expressed by all the other astrological signs. And yet they are neither this nor that; they are beyond the either-or. Most people cannot figure them out. Moses, who was born and died on the seventh day of Adar, was a Pisces. Moses was such a collective personality that he included all the diverse personalities of the Jewish people within himself. His inclusive disposition enabled him to be a leader. Moses was beyond either-or, and therefore he could bring God's Torah into the world—the Torah that supports and nurtures the revelation of God's oneness.

In our ordinary consciousness, we do not completely see or experience God's oneness, which transcends and permeates all. But on Purim, after a few drinks, it is amazing what we can see.

One of my teachers explained, in jest, that on any other day of the year, if you ask a drunkard how many fingers you are holding up and you show him two, he will likely see five, and if you show him one he will likely see three. But on Purim, if you show him two, he will see one, and if you show him five, he will see one. On Purim we see only one—the One.

On Purim we acknowledge God's absolute oneness and celebrate our trust in His ever-present love.

—TEN—

Conclusion

Love Is the Answer

Let us sum up what we have covered:

What are the Jewish Holy Days all about?

Love is the answer. Each Jewish Holy Day celebrates a vital aspect of God's timeless love for us.

Passover is the birthday of the Jewish people as a nation. On Passover we celebrate that God loves us unconditionally the way a father loves his child. In the name of unconditional love, God passed over His judgment and took our ancestors out of Egypt. Unconditional love, however, does have *one* condition, and that is that we acknowledge God's love and stand ready to accept it. Otherwise, we simply cannot experience it.

Shavuot celebrates the day our ancestors received the

Torah and its commandments (mitzvot) on Mount Sinai. Therefore, it can be described as the bar mitvzah of the Jewish people. The mitzvot nurture our relationship with God and enable us to express our true inner self, which is a spark of God. Whereas on Passover we celebrate freedom from oppression, on Shavuot we celebrate freedom of expression. We acknowledge that God lovingly empowers us to be His agents, to express our inner selves and accomplish on His behalf the sacred mission of overcoming evil, choosing goodness, and building this world.

The Talmud teaches that you cannot succeed in Torah until you fail in Torah. Sometimes we simply do not appreciate what we have till it's gone. On Tisha B'Av we acknowledge that we have failed in our mission. We express our deep sadness over the destruction of the Temple and painfully acknowledge the loss of God's presence from our lives. This tragic and mournful day inspires us to crave what really matters: love—love of God and for each other.

Accepting responsibility for our wrongdoings is the first step toward getting back on track to fulfill our mission and restoring God's presence to our lives. Therefore, on Rosh Hashanah, the Day of Judgment, we celebrate our accountability for our actions and rejoice over the fact that we are worthy to be judged. God loves us and our choices make a difference to Him.

On Yom Kippur, after we have regretted our wrongdoings and resolved to change our ways, we celebrate the power of forgiveness. We graciously accept God's forgiveness and forgive ourselves.

The cycle of the High Holidays is all about love. On Rosh Hashanah we are offered an opportunity to experience a higher level of consciousness in our eternal connection to God, unlike anything we have known before. With the blast of the shofar, we wake from our slumber—our unconscious, "back-to-back" connection to God—but we feel so small, insignificant, and embarrassed to face God.

From Rosh Hashanah to Yom Kippur we acknowledge our failings and bitterly regret distancing ourselves from God. These painful feelings, however, support, nurture, and empower us to ultimately face God. On Yom Kippur we return to face God and experience His loving forgiveness.

Once the load of our wrongdoings is off our heads, we joyfully prepare ourselves for the holiday of Sukkot. The challenge of judgment on Rosh Hashanah and the joy of forgiveness on Yom Kippur now enable us on Sukkot to confidently embrace God and feel embraced by God. The holiday of Sukkot is the "time of our happiness," because now we can celebrate our successful return to wholeness. We also reclaim our spontaneity and zest for life, which was inevitably lost during the arduous process that preceded it.

The unparalleled joy we feel throughout Sukkot can be best described as the joy of anticipation for the incredible, intimate experience of Simchat Torah, when we dance joyously with the Torah. On that great day we experience the ecstasy of knowing that God is one, and we are one with God and each other. Although Simchat

Torah is the ultimate experience of our intimate connection with God, the anticipation of this experience during Sukkot offers us the greatest joy.

On Rosh Hashanah we experience God as our Judge, on Yom Kippur we experience God as our forgiving Father, but on Sukkot we experience God as our Lover. Sukkot can be described as our wedding with God and Simchat Torah as the consummation of the marriage.

The miraculous possibilities of the intense love that we feel for God and from God are revealed on Chanukah. Chanukah commemorates the miraculous victory of the Jews over the mighty Greek army. However, it also celebrates the miracle of a small cruse of oil, holding only enough fuel for one day, somehow lasting and giving light for eight days. Celebrating this unnecessary miracle is the ultimate celebration of love.

In the light of Chanukah, we see that really everything is a miracle, because nothing necessarily has to be. We exist only by the grace of God and the free expression of His love. Because God loves us, anything is possible—so we should never lose hope.

Tu B'Shvat, known as the "new year for the trees," is an opportune time to celebrate how God's loving presence is also readily available even in the ordinary physical pleasures of this world. During the Tu B'Shvat feast, when we recite a blessing before we eat and acknowledge fruits as gifts from God, we taste God's loving presence within the physical and bring back the blessing to the earth.

Purim celebrates the ultimate revelation of God's

hidden oneness and ever-present love. It shows that His love is hidden in every event of our lives. On Purim we acknowledge that all exists within God and that, although we can do other than God's will, we can never oppose His plan. Therefore, God does not have to interfere with the events of history and do outright miracles to save us. Everything is in the hands of God, and whatever happens is all for the best. In the light of Purim, we are able to see that even the evil ones, who are determined to destroy us, actually end up revitalizing and rejuvenating us.

When we know that God's love for us is eternal and at the core of every situation of our lives, we can trust that God's love and care for us is hidden within every occurrence—good or bad—of our lives. It's all love. On Purim we celebrate the revelation of God's ever-present hidden love. Even in the most challenging and difficult moments, we know to trust God, because His love for us is unconditional—always and forever.

Invitation to the Reader

Dear Reader,

Please feel free to write me. It would be an honor and pleasure to receive your comments and questions.

All the best,
David Aaron

Isralight
25 Misgav Ladach
Old City, Jerusalem
97500
Israel

E-mail: david.aaron@isralight.org
Web site: www.rabbidavidaaron.com

About the Author

Rabbi David Aaron (www.rabbidavidaaron.com), the son of a Holocaust survivor, has struggled since early youth to understand and feel God's love and compassion. His own spiritual journey led him to Israel, where he studied Torah and Jewish mysticism under the tutelage of the great masters. He received his rabbinical ordination in 1979 from the Israel Torah Research Institute (Yeshivat ITRI). A popular lecturer in North America and a frequent guest on radio and TV, David Aaron is the founder and dean of Isralight (www.isralight.org), an international organization with programming throughout Israel, North America, and South Africa. Rabbi Aaron lives in Jerusalem with his wife, Chana, and their seven children.

David Aaron's other books include *Endless Light: The Ancient Path of the Kabbalah to Love, Spiritual Growth, and Personal Power* (1997, 1998), *Seeing God: Ten Life-Changing Lessons of the Kabbalah* (2001, 2002), and *The Secret Life of God: Discovering the Divine within You* (2004, 2005).